Effective
Meetings

Second Edition

SAGE HUMAN SERVICES GUIDES

A series of books edited by ARMAND LAUFFER and CHARLES D. GARVIN. Published in cooperation with the University of Michigan School of Social Work and other organizations.

Effective Meetings

Improving Group
Decision Making

Second Edition

John E. Tropman

SHSG SAGE HUMAN
SERVICES GUIDE 17

*Published in cooperation with the University
of Michigan School of Social Work*

SAGE Publications
International Educational and Professional Publisher
Thousand Oaks   London   New Delhi

HD
30
.23
.T73
1996

For information address:

SAGE Publications, Inc.
2455 Teller Road
Thousand Oaks, California 91320
E-mail: order@sagepub.com

SAGE Publications Ltd.
6 Bonhill Street
London EC2A 4PU
United Kingdom

SAGE Publications India Pvt. Ltd.
M-32 Market
Greater Kailash I
New Delhi 110 048 India

Printed in the United States of America

Library of Congress Cataloging-in-Publication Data

Tropman, John E.
   Effective meetings: Improving group decision making / John E. Tropman.—2nd. ed.
        p.   cm.   —(Sage human services guides; v. 17, 2nd. ed.)
   Includes bibliographical references.
   ISBN 0-7619-0020-9 (cloth: alk. paper).   —   ISBN 0-7619-0021-7 (pbk.: alk. paper).
      1. Meetings.   2. Committees.   3. Decision making, Group.
   I. Title.   II. Series.
   AS6.T73   1996
   658.4'56—dc20   95-35749

This book is printed on acid-free paper.

96 97 98 99   10 9   8   7   6   5   4   3   2   1

Production Editor: Diane S. Foster

CONTENTS

PREFACE TO THE FIRST EDITION

There are many cartoons about boards and committees, most suggesting that these groups accomplish little. One shows two men bending over their date books. One is saying, "Gee, if I can get in one more meeting this week, I won't have to do any work!" Another, by Charles Addams, shows a father and son walking in a plaza where there are statues of groups. The father says, "There are no great men, my boy, only great committees." The first cartoon represents part of our feelings about decision-making groups—that they waste time and that they accomplish little. Real work is not done there. The Addams cartoon, however, points out an uncomfortable truth. Group effort is necessary. There is pressure to "get on board," to "be a good team player." Despite the pressure, we have very little information about what to do once we are on board, a situation that may contribute to committee and board incompetence and ineptitude while at the same time reinforcing their importance. This book is aimed at helping people make that "one more committee" worthwhile for themselves and for the others there and at facilitating the decision-making task of the group.

The central focus is boards and committees within the human service field. In the public sphere, for example, departments of mental health bring people together in decision-making and advisory roles. New efforts at localized activity are coordinated through departments of social services. Area agencies on aging work with citizens' advisory groups in all of their decision-making activities. In the private realm, United Way agencies plan and conduct fund-raising campaigns, and when the campaigns are over, decide on allocations. These decisions are made through—and ratified by —committees. The list goes on and on. Most of what I say about the role of committees, the functioning of boards, and the problems they face applies to decision-making groups wherever they occur. The suggestions I will make apply to committees and boards in general.

Special thanks go to Armand Lauffer, series editor, who provided very useful feedback, and to Robert Myers of the United Way of Canada. That organization provided partial support for an early draft of some chapters, and Mr. Myers made many helpful comments. Harold R. Johnson provided continual support. Finally, Elmer J. Tropman provided encouragement and wisdom.

PREFACE TO THE SECOND EDITION

Since the publication of the first edition of this book, more research has been done on decision-making groups of all kinds (Carver, 1990; Goodman & Associates, 1986; Hackman, 1990; Houle, 1989; Ketchem & Trist, 1992; Schwartzman, 1989). Two of the basic truths expressed in the initial edition remain valid:

1. *Despite significant changes in perspective, decision-making groups continue to be the objects of scorn and derision in American society.* Committee meetings, especially, continue to be the butt of jokes and cartoons. This negative perception and commentary reflects a notion of collective decision making as inept. To add insult to injury, they are also seen as imprisoning members in interminable meetings that waste time, while producing little or nothing.

2. *A lot can be done to improve the situation.* The techniques mentioned in this guide have been used successfully by thousands (the first edition sold more than 10,000 copies), and I continue to receive comments and questions from readers and users.

What has changed since the initial edition? The context in which organizations exist and work is hugely different. Every organization—nonprofit, for profit, governmental—is seeking to do its work better, faster, cheaper. Organizations are experiencing intense competition regardless of field—price competition, speed competition, and quality competition. Also, the velocity of environmental change is increasing, as Toffler (1980, 1990) points out. Peter Vail (1989) talks about this environment as "permanent white water." In such an environment, "quick response teams" are a major asset.

The move from placid streams to permanent white water signals a second change. Perhaps because of contextual change, organizations themselves are being transformed. Our rigid organizational "craft"—the timeworn, rigid "canoelike" structure, with strict hierarchies—does not work in the new environment. We need something pliable, an organizational craft that can absorb the impact of the hidden rocks and rushing water without cracking open, a craft that will carry us along. The flatter, more "configured" organization is moving from hierarchy to teams, from spans of control to spans of communication.

A third change has been the development and acceptance of the quality movement by organizations throughout the United States. For those who begin on a quality journey, all aspects of the organization deserve inspection. Meetings—the activities of decision groups—become a central work process to look at in terms of efficiency, effectiveness, and continuous quality improvement (CQI). When decision groups have to meet again to achieve some result they should have achieved at the last meeting, that is "rework," a problem of efficiency. From an organizational point of view, such rework as a result of the meeting process is the same as rework from any process.

When decision groups work efficiently but on the wrong problem, that is an issue of effectiveness.

When groups work swiftly, on the right problem, but come up with decisions of poor quality, then there is the need for CQI.[1]

A fourth change is the emphasis on evaluation on the part of managers everywhere. The changed organizational context and the emphasis on quality support evaluative activities. The quality movement also argues for evaluation. Improvements in efficiency and effectiveness are not the only thing one works toward. Decisions are the product of decision-making group meetings. Therefore, the decisions themselves need to be evaluated. The analysis scheme for decision assessment that was offered in the first edition is updated and expanded here.

These four changes—competitive environment; flatter, more resilient organizational structures; and emphases on quality and evaluation—affect all organizations, including nonprofits and human service organizations. Cutbacks of federal support of the human service sector have become common. Much decision making is shifting to the states and localities, where different actors and different "customers" have different agendas. Competition for the voluntary dollar has greatly increased. Although many nonprofits and human service organizations are small, many are large. (In 1995, the United Way of America is a $3+ billion-a-year system; the Michigan Department of Social Services is a $5+ billion-a-year system). Many of these larger organizations are taking steps to simplify their structures, and the increased, efficient use of decision-making groups is a part of that change. In the nonprofit world, the United Way of America has its own quality award program for local United Ways. Human service organizations across the country are thinking more about customers than clients, looking carefully at what they do and how they do it—in short, taking evaluation seriously. (It matters what those who use services are called. *Customers* have a legitimate right to structure an organization's services and have something to say about those services, whereas *clients* are in a weaker position.)

But there are some changes that have had special impact on nonprofit and human service organizations. One is a recognition of the size of the sector (Tropman & Tropman, 1987). In 1977, there were 103,066 such organizations with one or more paid employee, and the number is surely larger now. If one includes an estimate for volunteer time, the case flow of the sector amounted to around $200 billion in 1983 dollars. Clearly, these are significant and central resources to American society, and they need to be managed well.

In addition, privatization of social service efforts has had a big effect on the nonprofit and human service sector. Additional special efforts to be "bottoms up" with respect to the disadvantaged and to be a leader in issues of diversity and inclusiveness have had a special effect on this group of organizations.

These changes have stimulated many intraorganizational realignments. Among them is a granting of respect for group activity and an increased emphasis on teams, groups, committees, task forces—self-managed units of all kinds. Despite the aforementioned snide remarks about committee meetings, group decision making is getting a lot of attention—the time it takes, the way it works, the possibility of improvement. Self-managed groups have moved from the periphery to the center of organizational life. The negativism is still there, but it has perhaps lessened and now must compete with respect for group-based activity. Hence there is more respect for decision-making groups and for the tools that help them to work well.

I hope this second edition contains the value of the old as well as the benefits of the new. It has been reorganized. Instead of the previous sequence of chapters, after Chapter 1, the book now appears in four parts.

Part I emphasizes "rules" for effective decision making. These rules provide a recipe of necessary ingredients for effective and efficient management of decision-making groups. Recruiting members (Chapter 2) is a first step. Chapter 3 details the needed preparations for decision group meetings, including rules of halves, three quarters, and some new rules. Chapter 4 deals with the agenda, a crucial management tool. The rule of the "agenda bell" is outlined here. Chapter 5 goes into the process of the meeting and suggests some techniques for helping the process move along.

Part II deals with positions. This material appeared in several different places in the first edition. Here, it is organized into chapters on the chair (Chapter 6), the member (Chapter 7), the staffer (Chapter 8), and the executive (Chapter 9).

Part III explores different kinds of groups. Many organizations have special concern with their boards, a group covered in Chapter 10. The chapter on the advisory committee was very popular in the previous edition, and it is expanded (Chapter 11). Many readers asked for a chapter on the staff meeting—a major time waster in many nonprofit and human service organizations (and other organizations too!). I am happy to oblige (Chapter 12).

Part IV considers two special topics: (a) ways to evaluate meetings with particular emphasis on the outcomes (decisions) and (b) techniques for developing a perspective on the importance of group decision making.

NOTE

1. Improving the meetings of decision-making groups, therefore, can be seen as an aspect of "work-out," which is the process of taking work (time and effort) out of the system. If, for example, it used to take a decision-making group five meetings to achieve some result and that result can now be achieved in three, the work-out consists of two fewer meetings.

ACKNOWLEDGMENTS

A second edition requires additional recognition. Armand Lauffer, as editor of this series, deserves special appreciation for his continual encouragement, support, and editorial assistance. Jim Nageotte, my editor at Sage, was unfailingly helpful and supportive.

Special thanks, as well, go to the many readers who have contacted me over the years. Some have suggested improvements and shared problems with applications, and others have spoken with me about what went right and wrong. Many readers liked the agenda bell and found it easy to use. Some wanted more attention devoted to total quality management. This current version includes these suggested improvements. My thanks to you all.

Dan Madaj, my editorial associate, worked with me to put the physical volume together. An author himself, his editorial judgment was always reliable. He added interest and vitality to the entire book.

Special thanks are due to my late father, Elmer J. Tropman. A human service professional, it was his early interest in committees that sparked my own interest in decision-making groups. His wisdom and perspective remain at the core of this work.

Each of my children contributed in special ways to this volume. Their reviews and comments were always helpful. Sarah's perspective on health groups, Jessica's knowledge of the library and information science field, and Matthew's experience with group decision-making styles in the field of music enriched my perspective immeasurably.

My wife, Penny, sustained me through this entire project, with intellectual support and critique as well as encouragement.

My thanks to you all.

INTRODUCTION

How often have you felt that just one more committee, one more group meeting, would push you over the edge? Somehow, decision groups seem not to "do work." Work is something individuals do. Attending meetings and working in groups is not work at all.

DECISION GROUPS
ARE PORTRAYED AS INEPT

Public references, as well as cartoons, repeatedly suggest that groups are collections of the impotent convened to do the impossible. A committee was once defined as a group that takes minutes to waste hours.

In any serious consideration of problems inherent in the group decision-making field, the negative view must be taken into consideration. One reason, of course, is to see if it is so. Are such groups really as incompetent as portrayed? What is most likely is that sometimes they are and sometimes they are not, which leads to questions about the conditions under which success and failure arise.

The second reason is to determine why, despite pervasive faults, decision groups are so omnipresent and so apparently "powerful." This power is not always expressed in terms of accomplishment but in terms of the groups' capacity to irritate, annoy, and cause downright anger. Particular hostility is reserved for the "weekly staff meeting." As one reader expressed it, "We meet every week for several hours. Nothing happens. People tune out or do not come. Then, because of low attendance, we have to meet again. It's insanity, but we can't seem to get off the meeting merry-go-round!"

No improvement in decision group functioning, however small, can occur unless we take these mechanisms of collective decision making seriously. If we continue to view them as time wasting or as peripheral to the work of an organization (or, for that matter, to modern society), then we will continue to waste personal resources, "putting in time" in decision group meetings and activity as a sort of public penance.

Why are meetings so disliked and at the same time so hard to reform, to improve? There are several reasons, and an understanding of these reasons is essential if we are to begin on the pathway to better meetings.

INDEPENDENCE VERSUS INTERDEPENDENCE

One part of the answer is cultural. North American cultural values tend to support individual action over group activity, "mountain men" over "wagon trains" (even though wagon trains were, in many ways, more important). We think of North American society as having been built by "rugged individualists." Decision groups run counter to the mythology of individualistic decision making. The hero in the North American society—from Superman to Wonder Woman to Sergeant Preston—is the individual acting alone, deciding alone, the ruler of his or her own domain. Any social mechanism that suggests group interdependence, such as the decision group, is likely to be negatively viewed for precisely this reason. North Americans in general and U.S. Americans in particular hesitate to acknowledge situations in which interdependence with others is an important and necessary part of their lives.

UBIQUITY

A second point is the ubiquity of decision groups. It is bad enough that we should sometimes be forced to be interdependent; if we have to be interdependent everywhere, if groups sprout like mushrooms at every turn, our irritation grows apace. It seems impossible to avoid such associations. Indeed, it may be that their "everywhereness" is a sort of antidote to the strong strain of independence just mentioned. After all, groups do provide a sense of membership and meaning. Time after time, when I talk with executives and staff members about that noxious weekly staff meeting, they say that although they rarely get anything done, "It is good to get together, to get a chance to see each other, and to catch up!" It seems there may be a confusion of purpose.

SOCIAL DEBIT AND CREDIT

Interdependence and ubiquity are not the only generators of the negative image. Perhaps as powerful is the enmeshing uncertainty of commitment when joining a committee or a board. Negative, hostile humor about board incompetence is in part a cover for the very real demands of decision groups—demands of time, energy, and, sometimes, demands to change our views and "go along." We all recognize that there is some element of communal responsibility in group membership, yet we are often unsure what this might involve. Rural American society, for example, has long been praised for its fellowship and willingness to be helpful. The famous cup of sugar example is perhaps most often cited. One *could* go next door to borrow a cup of sugar from a neighbor if one happened to be out of sugar. What is less frequently observed, although not less frequently true, is that one was expected to pay back what one borrowed. The uncertainty was how. The borrower may feel that a cup of sugar is sufficient repayment. However, the lender may not need a cup of sugar but, rather, may make some other demand on the borrower. What might be demanded and when? Payment might be requested at an inconvenient time or in a coin that the borrower does not wish to part with. Uncertainty clouds the picture. The old phrase "neither a borrower nor a lender be" seems to apply as much to the network of social obligations as it does to the simple and well-defined borrowing of money at a predetermined rate of interest. Financial debit, of course, is preferable to "social debit" because the terms are well understood.

Joining a decision group or board involves this fundamental uncertainty. One sits with others to make decisions. In so doing, one invariably becomes indebted or committed to other members. It is not clear whether payment will be demanded, and, in fact, payment may be demanded in a way (through a vote or support of a proposal one would otherwise dislike) that is viewed negatively by the particular member in question. Hence decision groups and boards represent a substantial amount of uncertainty to the individual members who recognize that commitments increase, that debts pile up, and that the decision group and board arena is one place where they may be discharged. On the other hand, requests may be difficult or impossible to meet, thus putting a member in a very stressful position. This stressful uncertainty may lead to the depiction of decision groups and boards as ineffective. Through humorous attacks, such portrayals attempt to deny the claim they make on individuals, not in terms of the particular decision but in terms of the social obligations, the social network, and the communal commitments inherent in decision group and board membership.

Perhaps the need to downplay these commitments and entanglements is one reason that the decision group is portrayed as a place where nothing gets done and no one has much effect. A central reason for decision group disdain lies in the reassurance that such disdain gives the individual members comfort that they have not violated norms of independence. It also provides comfort for them that if the group were to take some action, that action would not really matter anyway. Indeed, because decision groups can act in some way that commits or otherwise encumbers the individual members, members are restive about them.

The reality is that decisions—good and poor—made at staff meetings, board meetings, and Parent-Teacher Association (PTA) meetings are made by decision groups. These decisions involve the members in ways that intrude on other aspects of their lives. It is that intrusion, that possibility that the member might, indeed, have to defend a decision he or she did not like or publicly agree with something he or she did not privately support, that causes discomfort within the ranks.

LACK OF PSYCHOLOGICAL
AND SKILL-BASED TRAINING
FOR WORK IN DECISION GROUPS

The North American mythology that the individual can go it alone does not support the notion of training and skills for communal activity. Other societies, for example, Japanese society, where these realities are better recognized, do a better job than North America in preparing people for communal decision making. Those who have contact with global companies frequently reflect on how different North Americans are in this insistence on individualism. For this reason, special preparation may be needed for decision groups and their participants.

In fact, two kinds of preparation are needed. One kind of training is the psychological preparation for group involvement. It must be seen as vital, central, and potentially more productive than individual, lonely-at-the-top approaches. This acceptance requires a social-psychological frame of reference that accepts the values of mutuality in decision making. Part of the preparation for successful decision group activity is the realization that both individualism and collectivism, both singleness and groupness have a place within modern complex society.

A 1994 issue of the *Harvard Business Review* tells the story about trouble in the team. The trouble was that someone assigned to the team did not believe in teams at all. The troublesome person refused to participate helpfully in group activities and actually devalued the work of others. An explosion occurred, and the person commented,

"A brilliant idea never came out of a *team*. Brilliant ideas come from brilliant individuals, who then inspire others in the organization to implement them.

> . . . I want this company to succeed as much as you do, but I believe, and I believe passionately, that groups are useless. Consensus means mediocrity. I'm sorry, but it does." (Wetlaufer, 1994, pp. 25-26)

Whatever other skills he had, clearly, he lacked the psychological preparation for group membership.

The second kind of training, the elements emphasized in this book, focus on tactics and techniques for managing and facilitating effective decision group activity. There are concrete skills that can help meetings go better, participants feel better, and results track toward high quality. At some point, all of us will serve on decision groups, task forces, or boards. Many of us will be called on to fill specific positions—to lead a subdecision group or serve as chair or secretary. We need to know how to influence the process from a participant's point of view as well as a chair's point of view. I hope this book will serve some of these purposes. We should all know about decision group management. One more decision group may indeed be all we need—to get the job done!

Chapter 1

THE MODERN DECISION GROUP

Bill Walker and Travis Smith were talking after the weekly board meeting of Bootstrap, Inc., a local voluntary agency.

"I don't know why these meetings are so bad," Bill said.

"Me either," said Travis. "They go on and on, and everybody seems to want to put his oar in."

"It's the same on a couple of other boards that I'm on," Bill said, "They seem to be in trouble all the time."

"Now that you mention it, it's the same at work too," Travis added. "My weekly production meeting never gets anything done, but we always must have it, it seems."

"Still," Bill said, "we can't do it all ourselves."

"You're right," said Travis. "And with all the competition today, we have to engage in more collaborative efforts. Unless we do better at meetings, we will never survive!"

Today's nonprofits live in an increasingly complex society. More and more, groups, teams, and committees are the center of decision-making activity. Most organizational actions and decisions are reviewed or actually created by one or more decision groups. This is true whether within the organization or in the midst of the interorganizational network. As we move into the 21st century, increasing numbers of decision groups are needed to handle our daily business.

EFFECTIVE DECISION MAKING

Decision groups are formed for one purpose only, to make decisions. There are, of course, other kinds of groups—social or personal groups formed for a variety of purposes. These groups are legitimate. Yet we should distinguish very carefully between the functions and purposes that groups do have. Even fact-finding groups are set up to make decisions about facts. If a group is set up to make decisions, as decision groups are, then everything done within the group should be aimed toward enhancing and facilitating the making of those decisions. To this end, I hope this guide will be of assistance. Part of the process of decision group management is to be aware of the social needs members have and address them without being consumed by them. This volume offers a perspective somewhat different from that which readers may find in other discussions on decision groups. The most common material picks up on the difficulties in functioning that many of these groups have and then begins to attribute them to the personalities of the members. Often, cartoons depict Arthur Angry pounding the table, Silent Selma withdrawing into the corner, Turbulent Terry jumping up and down and spilling his coffee, Dick Director acting decisively. These caricatures are portrayed with the hope that one can either see oneself or identify the problem people.

Implicit in this kind of analysis, and frequently explicit in the suggestions for improvement, is a series of remedies that involve shaping the personalities of such members or, failing that, removing them in some overt or subtle way. Yet after one has spent a good bit of time in the decision group and board activity realm, it becomes clear that personality is less important than one initially thought. When one Arthur Angry is removed, someone else takes his place. From a structural perspective, one is forced to look at the extent to which elements of the group structure may be as responsible for decision group and board problems as are the personalities of the members. That is the perspective offered here.

It takes into account both "rules" and "positions." I'll explain. Reflect for a moment on how little education or training has been available for the kinds of decision group activities that are so common and so crucial today. Typically, such information is picked up informally, usually through some kind of apprentice experience with a person whom we regard as a good chair or good decision group member. There is so little teaching done that when a group of us got together and wrote a book called *The Essentials of Committee Management* (Tropman, Johnson, & Tropman, 1979), many of the publishers found themselves unable to take it seriously. One wrote back to say, "You're not seriously offering us a book on committee groups, are you?" adding that his "executive decision group" had rejected the manuscript. We were serious. That book, accepted by another publisher, is now in *its* second edition also, slightly retitled as *Committee Management in the Human Services* (Tropman, Johnson, & Tropman, 1992). That book and the first edition of this book offer twin perspectives on making improvements in decision-making groups. One focuses on rules to help things go better. The other emphasizes positions in such groups and the things we need to know and do when we are in these positions (such as chair and member).

A rules perspective suggests that there are some relatively simple rules or "recipes" involving the details of preparation for a decision group meeting that can immensely enhance the productivity of the meeting.

Similarly, the positions perspective suggests that crucial positions are to be played within the decision group framework and that frequently people have almost no idea about what these positions are—except in the most general sense—or how to play them. Typically, little thought has been given to position flexibility and facility. Most of the time, we shift from one position to another as we move through the day—sometimes a chair, sometimes a member, sometimes providing staff and executive service to a group, and then back again to chair. These changes in positions are rarely accompanied by actual changes in behavior. Even when people know what is expected of them, they may not know what behaviors will achieve these expectations.

Much needs to be done before we even get to the meeting at which decisions are to be made. A more complete knowledge of what the positions involve and a more discerning application of them will result in vastly enhanced decision group performance.

The meeting itself is an end point in a long series of activities, rather than the beginning point. Once the meeting begins, the course of events is heavily influenced by what has or has not happened before it began. The best opportunities for influence and structuring exist during that premeeting period. Once the meeting has begun, it is generally too late.

Contrary to what many think is true, personality is not as important as knowing one's position. It is not so much how charismatic or powerful we are, as it is whether we learn the role for our position and play it correctly. This approach uses the perspective developed by Erving Goffman (1959) in his book *The Presentation of Self in Everyday Life*. He looks at life as a play and people as the actors in that play. Hence the meeting can be seen as the performance of a play—sometimes a history, sometimes a drama, sometimes a comedy, sometimes all three! If the decision group meeting is seen as a play and the decision group members as players, then everyone needs a script (and the script can allow for improvisation). Everyone has to know his or her position or role, and everyone has to play that role properly.

But a performance is not good enough unless it achieves a goal; a good meeting must be more than entertainment. It must achieve purpose. The point is to make excellent decisions, not just "any old decision." All too often, groups—through impatience, exhaustion, irritation—are satisfied with any decision. Participants are so grateful to avoid chaos and get something done that they pay little attention to whether that something is of high quality. Thus we will be looking not only at the rules for and positions in decision group participation but also at the results of those processes. After all, if decision groups are assembled to make decisions, then the true measure of decision group performance is not whether the room was well ventilated or whether the coffee arrived on time, however important these props to the setting of the committee stage are. Rather, we should look at the decision itself and ask, Is it a good decision? Is it a poor decision? Are we possibly worse off after we made the decision than we were before the decision was made?

WHY DECISION GROUPS
DON'T ALWAYS WORK WELL

Decision groups don't work well because four elements of quality decision group function are not addressed.

Basic Perspectives for
High-Quality Decision Group Meetings

- Set expectations aimed at accomplishment.
- Provide scripts (agendas).
- Inform participants about positions requirements.
- Strive for high-quality decisions (see Exercise 1.1 at the end of this chapter).

Unless these elements are brought in, decision group competence gives way to decision group chaos. Expectations are not set; scripts are not available; people are ignorant about their positions, and they fail to strive for high-quality decisions. These challenges represent additional superordinate problems with which decision groups must deal. They are often a step removed from the actual apparent problem, the nitty-gritty difficulty of planning the church supper or developing a social plan for the PTA this year.

Michael Cohen and James G. March (1974) suggest four additional reasons for problems in group functioning, which I have adapted for use here:

Low salience
High inertia
Burnout
Decision overload

I'll explain what they mean.

Low Salience. The bulk of decision group work is of low salience. Decisions that are relatively trivial in nature are brought to the agenda. Frequently, management problems within the decision group lend these decisions great importance. Whether we should have square or round waste baskets is a topic that can consume a great deal of attention. One person has reported a meeting that involved the approval of popcorn poppers for a PTA. Somebody said that they had better get a popcorn popper that would pop all the kernels because she had broken her tooth on an unpopped kernel! Another member added, "Well, it wasn't really the popper, it was really the oil" and began to suggest proper oils for popping corn. A third member then added that it wasn't really the popper or the oil, it was the corn itself and began recommending a famous brand. When still another individual added that it was really neither the oil nor the corn but the heat, the meeting collapsed into decision group chaos. Here was a group of community leaders, having taken time out of a busy day to do some important work, sitting around discussing how to pop corn! It can drive even the most dedicated decision group member crazy. We therefore need to think about the ways in which items of low salience can be handled quickly and items of greater salience can be given proper attention.

High Inertia. Decision groups often suffer from high inertia. Like the water buffalo, they are hard to get going and hard to stop. Therefore, it is appropriate to have a set of procedures that make decision group start-up easier, with particular attention to initial meetings and the preparation for them, as well as ways in which decision groups can be terminated.

Burnout. Decision groups become subject to burnout. A self-fulfilling prophecy is created by the decision group environment. A decision group perceived as an effective decision-making body is likely to be asked to do more (as are individuals who are perceived to be effective decision makers). At a certain point, without proper techniques of agenda management and mission control, the decision group may have more to do than it can reasonably accomplish. The result is that it may begin not to do things that people expect of it. You've probably witnessed more than one effective decision group struggling under such a load that it rapidly sinks into incompetence. At that point, people—frequently the same ones who made the additional requests in the first place—point out that decision groups, after all, cannot do anything. But it may be too late for the decision group.

Decision Overload. Cohen and March (1974) suggest that decisions tend to become "Christmas trees"—one decision can become a place to hang all other decisions, amendments, and emendations. Rather than partializing the problem, decisions become overloaded. Of course, the more issues and problems that are hung on any particular decision, the less likely that decision is to be made or made well. It may have to satisfy too many people. But such problems can be solved. Decision group functions can be managed and managed effectively. Quality decisions can be made (see Exercise 1.2 at the end of this chapter).

It is my belief that decision group performance can be vastly improved through the appropriate use of a set of decision group management techniques and through the appropriate application of a set of position prescriptions. Step away from the simplistic diagnoses of Tommy Talkalot and Oliver Obstructionist and move toward making the decision group a crucial decision-making group, one whose performance can be improved and efficiency enhanced.

CONCLUSION

The primary aim of decision groups is to actually make decisions. This is most effectively accomplished when preliminary structuring has been done and when members know their positions. Good decisions accelerate decision group effectiveness.

Bill and Travis continued talking.

"I know what you mean, Bill," Travis offered. "Still, it seems that something ought to be done; there ought to be some way that we could improve these meetings."

"Good point," said Bill. "You know, someone told me about a film he had seen about meetings and results. Maybe we should get that film and show it. That could help. And if we gave the members a few things to read, maybe that would help too. What do you think?"

"Not right away," Travis said. "We need to read a few things ourselves first. Then let's see if there are some exercises we can convince the group to try out."

EXERCISE 1.1

BASIC PERSPECTIVES FOR
HIGH-QUALITY DECISION GROUP MEETINGS

Think of a decision group (board, committee, task force) you participate in. Then think about the following questions in relationship to it.

1. Set expectations aimed at accomplishment.
   Were accomplishment-oriented expectations expressed? How and why (or why not?)
2. Provide scripts (agendas)
   Were basic scripts (agendas) made available? Why or why not?
3. Inform participants about positions requirements.
   Did participants understand their positions? Why or why not?
4. Strive for high-quality decisions.
   Were high-quality decisions made? Were *any* decisions made?

EXERCISE 1.2

PROBLEMS IN FUNCTIONING

Michael Cohen and James G. March (1974) suggest four additional reasons for problems in functioning: (a) low salience, (b) high inertia, (c) decision group overload, and (d) decision overload.

Consider some of the decision groups you have participated in, either as a member or chair. If things went badly, to what extent did Cohen and March's (1974) generalizations reflect the situation as you faced it?

Low salience
High inertia
Burnout
Decision overload

PART I

Rules for Effective
Group Decision Making

The four chapters in Part I focus on essential rules for running good decision-making groups. What "good" means in this context is that the right people are brought together with the needed information to make decisions of high quality, decisions that advance the mission and purpose of the nonprofit organization or human service coalition sponsoring the group. Several elements of "good" need to be considered. The "right" individuals for the group cannot always be determined unless one has some idea of the topics to be considered. On the other hand, creative and engaged participants change the very definition of the problem. Hence there is a dynamic interaction between the participants and the issues. Recruitment is key.

But blending these elements is important as well. Also important for success are a number of "mechanics" for preparing the meeting. After securing the people and information needed, one has to get all of them in the same room at the same time. This is the premeeting, or preparatory, phase—the phase that no one wants to take responsibility for. And if you do it, you don't get much credit for it.

In fact, there are those who see planning as constraining. However, the reverse is usually true. You get credit if the meeting goes well, and you are regarded as having managed it well. But as I noted, most of what members think of as management *in* the meeting really depends on careful work *before* the meeting.

Most consultants agree that there is a 1 to 4 leverage factor in planning; every hour spent in planning saves 4 hours later. My own experience affirms that this ratio is more correct than not; the group that gets together with no agendas, "just to explore issues," often ends up meeting many times again, because the exploration, which could have been started and organized in a preliminary way before the meeting, creates a chaotic situation that then adds its own difficulties to an already difficult situation. Simple rules help here.

The agenda is one of the most important tools for developing and organizing the prework and assisting in the meeting itself. For this reason, an entire chapter is devoted to the agenda, looking at its overall structure, the ways in which it can be configured to assist in both planning and execution, and the specific ways in which it might be written to maximize communication. One of the most popular elements of the previous edition—the "agenda bell"—is outlined here.

Finally, we move into the meeting itself. All the preparation in the world will not make a decision group function well. Lack of preparation can destroy a meeting, but intrameeting elements need to be attended to as well.

Chapter 2

RECRUITMENT OF PARTICIPANTS

Francine Smith, head of the AIDS Hotline, was talking with one of the staff members. "I don't know," said Francine, "how to make our monthly staff meetings more appealing. I have invited our staff and the staffs from community mental health, the visiting nurses association, the local hospitals, and others who need to be informed about AIDS Hotline activities. But sometimes they come, and sometimes they don't."

Jessica Namport, a staffer, had long been concerned about these meetings. It seemed everyone and their sister, brother, and parents was on the invitation list. She had to get the list out and make the preparations. They always planned for 45 people, but only 8 or 9 came. She was frustrated. "I get lots of calls asking what the meeting is about," commented Jessica. "And you know, the agenda is the same, week after week—a report from this group, a report from that group."

"Perhaps there is a way we could create a bit more focus. I hate these meetings as much as you do, Jessica," said Francine, "but it's good to have them even if just a few come."

If all the world's a stage, then getting the right actors becomes a crucial task for the meeting planner. All too frequently, decision group membership is offered for the "wrong" reasons, such as choosing by position or choosing to fill out racial or gender categories (although such motives will almost always be denied in public as frequently as they are acknowledged in private). Sometimes, as Cohen, March, and Olsen (1972) suggest, membership is chosen almost at random, as if the membership was tossed into a "garbage can" (see Chapter 5). Or people come to meetings as a substitute for someone else who is a participant but cannot be there. Sometimes it's simply power. Powerful people get to go; others do not, regardless of whether the powerful person should not be there and the less powerful one should be.

These wrong reasons do have a place: Offices do need a presence; racial and gender considerations are vital for a diverse set of perspectives on decision making. Power is vital, but so is information.

Despite the fact that most of us tend to think in terms of the categories of *people,* what is more important are the categories of *information.* Fundamentally, participation needs to be driven by mission. What needs to be done determines who needs to be at the meeting. If mission is the key driver in general, then the agenda should be the key driver in particular.

MEMBERSHIP BY MISSION

All decision groups need a charter. A charter outlines the purpose of the group, and from that purpose the overall selection of team members, participants, associates, players, or whatever is made. As the contemporary saying has it, "If you don't know where you're going, any road will take you there." Similarly, "If you don't know why you're meeting, any participants will do." The operative phrase should be *purpose drives participants.*

Purpose in this case is not defined by phrases such as "the staff meeting" or "the board meeting." The charter must spell out the group's intentions, goals, contributions to mission, or whatever is the assignment. Most boards would greatly benefit from such specification. It would help them select the kinds of people they need and help focus the kinds of information they consider and problems they discuss.

Much the same could be said for the generally awful staff meetings. Staff meetings rate a new chapter in this edition simply because they are so universally disliked by executives and other staff members. Purpose clarifies focus, and such clarification allows membership to be selected appropriately. In the AIDS Hotline example mentioned earlier, there is no clear mission, and hence the invitation list is a laundry list.

LEVELS OF MEMBERSHIP

Often, people mistakenly think that one is either a "member" or "not a member" of a group. That false assumption would mean all those who might ever be needed better be added in the beginning, because unless they are members they will not be able to "buy in." Because offices are often thought to be essential, when individuals who are head of the member office cannot come they send subordinates, whose usual contribution is "I can't say anything until I check with my boss!"

An alternative approach begins with the concept of levels of membership—standing, temporary, informal or semiformal insiders, informal or semiformal outsiders, and staffers. Additional categories could be apprentices, juniors, and emeriti.[1]

Standing Members. Standing members can be considered the *cadre* of the decision group. The military sense of that term means, loosely, "the permanent members assigned to a base." These would be the core members of an orchestra, the basic corps de ballet, the folks who are needed regularly, who are deeply involved, and who are required for the functioning of the group. These individuals are selected as most central to the mission. For example, in the AIDS Hotline group, time should be spent thinking about what the purpose of the group actually is. That would enable a cadre of membership to be identified. Jessica could work on them as her central priority.

Temporary Members. At various times in the lives of decision groups, special projects and issues come up. When that happens, temporary members might be added to the group for easy access to their knowledge and expertise. Consider the AIDS Hotline. One of the problems these hotlines have is the obscene phone caller. Let's say that one of the group's projects was the installation of equipment to record such calls. During the development and implementation of that project, technicians (and relevant others) might be added to the group as temporary members.

Informal or Semiformal Insiders. Sometimes, individuals with information that might be useful for a decision group join the group on an informal basis—for example, a support staff person or an accountant. *Informal* here can mean regular or on request. This arrangement is fine as long as their status is clear to those who join the group on this basis and clear to the standing members.

Informal or Semiformal Outsiders. There are other times when individuals outside the organization might be added to a decision group. This often occurs when there are the so-called upstream or downstream dependencies. For example, if a counseling agency gets referrals from a community mental health center and this source of referrals is crucial to the functioning of the agency, then someone from that "source" agency might well be included as an informal or semiformal outsider, bringing information and perspective to the decision group. The same point could be made on the downstream side. For example, if a hospital "refers out" to a particular nursing home, it might be good to have an informal connection to that home, so that the hospital is not suddenly caught with a problematic change of policy or the like.

Staffers. Staffers are individuals hired to assist the decision group in carrying out its functions. The staffer position is a complex one, and a whole chapter will be devoted to it (as well as to the executive, a special kind of staffer.) When a group is formed (say, to search for new staffers, find a new executive, or design next year's budget) and someone is assigned *to provide staff service* to that group, the staffer is not a member of the group, but is a regular insider or outsider.

Apprentices. Sometimes, students or learners are assigned to sit with a decision group. Often, they perform simple "staff services" in exchange for the opportunity to observe and learn.

Juniors. Juniors are younger staff members or newer staff members, insiders or outsiders, who might be playing some role in the cadre in the future. For example, new operators at the AIDS Hotline might be invited to one or another of the meetings.

Emeriti. For some decision groups—boards, for example—there are current members, members-to-be, and past members. The emeriti are past members who, for specific purposes, may join a current meeting. They would be considered a temporary member, joining for a designated purpose.

THE MEMBERSHIP CALL

Once the central purpose is identified or clarified, individuals throughout the organization who could contribute or who are needed can also be identified. Other categories of membership, as just discussed, are also available.

But whom do you ask? Cohen et al. (1972) suggest that the specific picks are driven by what's on the agenda, both the short-term, one-meeting-type items and the long-term strategic items. Basically, they suggest that organizations have four kinds of people in them: problem knowers, solution providers, resource controllers, and decision makers looking for work. *Problem knowers* are those individuals—secretaries, receptionists, or janitors, for example—who know the problems the organization is facing. *Solution providers* are those creative people, who exist in all organizations among professional and lay membership, who have great ideas about what to do about problems once they know the problems. If they are not brought together with problem knowers, however, they may go off and solve some-one else's problem or some irrelevant problem. *Resource controllers*, usually middle managers, often neither know the problems the organization is facing nor have any ideas about what to do about them. But they control the allocation of people and money, resources that are likely to be vital to any developing solution. They need to be included in the loop. Finally, there are the *decision makers looking for work* who need to give the final blessing to ideas about projects and programs if those projects and programs are to move forward. They need to be in the loop early on.

Cohen and colleagues make the point that for high-quality decisions to occur, the relevant individuals for the problem at hand all need to be in the same room at the same time. Jessica's time would be better spent develop-ing an agenda and then working with Francine to let people know about the items on which their input was vital. That would make a lot more sense to them.

A problem, and perhaps *the problem*, is that people in the agency and the community do not come identified as problem knowers, solution providers, resource controllers, or decision makers. The people who can play these parts have to be found. But at least there is a start; we now know the relevant categories to look for.

CONCLUSION

The right membership is crucial if decision-making groups are to be successful. But the right people are only right for the right problem. Therefore, problems and issues must be specified in advance. General specification—the purpose principle—allows us to identify a general class of members who will fit the purpose we are about. Then, projects allow us to involve temporary members and informal or semiformal insiders or outsiders on an as-needed basis. Continued attention needs to be paid to people who know the problems of the organization, those who can create solutions, those who control resources, and those who need to bless the final product (see Exercise 2.1 at the end of this chapter).

Jessica thought to herself how much better the staff meeting was going now. She and Francine had gotten together and prepared a purpose. Information exchange was one such purpose, but that now occurred only once every 3 months. People had started to come to meetings. She had gotten some of the agenda items from the larger list (i.e., interests and concerns of the larger mem-bership expressed to her ahead of time) and could now include those items when appropriate. It seemed so much better she could hardly believe it.

NOTE

1. I would like to thank Professor Merle Crawford of the University of Michigan for suggesting some of the categories in this membership array.

EXERCISE 2.1

THE PURPOSES AND FUNCTIONS OF MEMBERSHIP

Think of a decision group on which you are currently serving. Consider the following questions:

Does the group have a written purpose? If not, why not? Could you prepare one?

Prepare a purpose, if only for your personal use. Then look at the categories of membership discussed in the chapter and reallocate people now on the list of members to these categories. Be sensitive, too, to the need to add members where categories are missing.

	Functions			
Categories	Problem	Solution	Resource	Decision
Standing members				
Temporary members				
Informal or semiformal insiders				
Informal or semiformal outsiders				
Staffer(s)				
Apprentices				
Juniors				
Emeriti				

Chapter 3

PREPARATIONS FOR
EFFECTIVE DECISION MAKING

The board of the Musical Therapy Society should have begun its meeting at 8:00. It is now 8:30, and the president is still not there. The society was set up with private and public funds to plan small concerts for homebound and institutionalized populations and to arrange for those who could not get out to attend musical performances. They also helped those who needed music lessons but could not afford them. There were many functions, and Bea Sharpe, a longtime member, was furious. Suddenly, the door flew open and the president bolted in, followed by a minicam from the local television station.

The president was in a state of panic. He turned to the group and said, "The television people say that this is an open meeting, that the law says we must have open meetings. They are going to film us for the news." At that, his folder with the evening's material slipped, and the first picture the television people got was a rear end shot of the president, picking up papers that had spilled over the table and onto the floor.

Bea covered her face. "Good Lord," she thought, "If orchestras played the way we have meetings, it would be chaos. Not only do we not start on time, but we wander all over the lot, we never have material on time, and often the most important items don't come until most of the people are gone. What a mess."

Perhaps the best way to look at the decision group is to conceive of it as an orchestra that comes together periodically to give certain performances for the public. When one thinks of it in this way, the amount of preparation that is required becomes more clear. Months before an orchestral performance, the score is chosen, the hall selected, seats divided up, and tickets sold. Advertisements and notices are sent out, and various kinds of equipment are brought together. The orchestra members have received copies of the scores and studied them; indeed, one of the functions of the orchestra manager is to see to it that everybody has copies of all of the music to be played and that no one is missing a page or two in the middle of one of the symphonies. In fact, a tremendous amount of preparation has been done so that all is in readiness when the orchestra gives its actual performance.

MAINTAINING FOCUS

Much of what happens at a meeting is determined before the meeting even begins. This simple fact is not appreciated by someone rushing into a meeting and saying, "Well, what's on the agenda?"

The key point is preparation. Think of your meeting as if it were an orchestra. Once the night and time of the performance have arrived, it is almost too late to do anything new or different from what has been prepared for. If one has not rehearsed, if the hall is not ready, if the instruments are not there, there is likely to be chaos rather than symphony. That, too, is fairly typical of many of our decision group performances. Just as an orchestral performance is governed by a score, so must a decision group follow the rules if it is to move smoothly and in concert toward a decision.

Five rules help focus the decision group on its task and anchor it in its mission.

Rules for Maintaining Focus
- Agenda integrity
- Temporal integrity
- The rule of halves
- The rule of thirds
- The rule of three quarters (see Exercise 3.1 at the end of this chapter)

Following these rules will be of great assistance in structuring decision group activity. I'll begin with discussion of the two integrity rules.

INTEGRITY

Agenda Integrity. Agenda integrity is a simple concept but hard to enforce. It suggests that it is the job of the chair and the duty of the decision group to see to it that two things occur:

1. All items on the agenda are discussed in the meeting for which they are scheduled.
2. No items not on the agenda are discussed.

Although it is permissible to touch base with a new item briefly or to give less than complete attention to an older item, it has been shown repeatedly that commitment to agenda integrity is necessary to ensure that time and effort are properly invested. Without it, important decisions may be deferred or left unmade. Moreover, lack of integrity can take the heart out of the participants. If, for example, you stay up half the night reading the AIDS Hotline report and then come to the meeting the next day only to find that the report was not to be discussed, it might be the last time that you make that kind of investment. And quite correctly—the decision group has given you the message that your homework was in vain. Similarly, in school, if the teacher is not going to cover the lesson, then the student is not going to do the homework. It is as simple as that.

Many chairs and members complain that nobody reads the material that was sent out—one of the most common problems that decision groups have. I run into it again and again in decision group counseling. As I explore the problem, participants tell me, "I don't read it because we never discuss it," or "We never discuss it when it's scheduled," or "I was not sent the new information that makes the old material obsolete, so I wasted my time."

It is essential, therefore, for chairs and members to stay with the agenda in front of them. This, of course, means that there needs to *be* an agenda in the first place (more on this later). A meeting without an agenda is like an orchestra without a score. No one knows what to do; no one knows where to go. Agenda integrity is impossible without an agenda. So as you go about decision group business, insist that a fairly complete agenda be prepared and be available; then insist that it be followed, and see to it that items not on the agenda do not intrude into the meeting itself. This can usually be accomplished by an application of the rule of halves, to be discussed later.

Let me explain why it is so important that you commit yourself to agenda integrity. Most of the time, items brought before decision groups are complex and difficult in nature. They require information for a decision to be made. Typically, somebody has merely heard on the way into the meeting that the governor's report is out. It is brought up at the meeting and people become very concerned. But in point of fact, no one has heard the governor's report; no one knows what the governor's report says; no one knows whether it even applies in the instance. If it does apply, no one is sure about the nature, extent, and other implications that such an application might have. Therefore, it is best not to discuss it at all. It can simply be announced, "There is a report, it has been heard, and we'll look into it." The announcement approach recognizes the concern that late-breaking items represent, while at the same time it does not add to the agenda items about which there is no information and for which people can share only ignorance.

The main purpose of making an agenda is to create a situation in which material can be prepared and the individual members can have the opportunity to make ready to consider the items. The late-breaking item that intrudes into the agenda disrupts that agenda, weakens the preparation that people have already done, and, typically, creates a situation in which discussion occurs without knowledge. That decision group members participate in this discussion in no way changes their criticism of the decision group process for spending time on such matters.

Agenda integrity, therefore, is the rule that says, "Handle those matters on the agenda; bring other matters up at other meetings." If it is a fast-breaking or late-breaking item, it can be held over for an emergency meeting the next day. It can be handled by a small group, or it can be handled, if necessary, by phone. In other words, there are alternative ways to handle an item such as this. To intrude it into an ongoing process is analogous to an orchestra playing a set piece when somebody from the audience shouts out, "I'd love to hear Symphony No. 40 by Mozart!" The orchestra stops and begins to play it; however, because not everyone knows it and there are no scores available, it sounds awful. People then say, "Gee, they really did terribly on that Mozart." We have to protect ourselves against ourselves.

Rules for Agenda Integrity
- There is an agenda.
- All agenda items are discussed.
- Items not on the agenda are not discussed.

Temporal Integrity. Have you heard the story of the man running down the street? He bumped into a friend, and the friend asked, "What's your hurry?" "I've got to get to my psychiatrist. If I don't get there on time, he starts without me."

The rule of temporal integrity is a shorthand way of saying, "Begin on time and end on time." Perhaps you've observed that most meetings start late and end late. Running late, we have to "catch up," cheating ourselves of the opportunity to proceed thoughtfully through an agenda. The rule of temporal integrity also suggests that some items ought to be scheduled before others and some given more time than others. Frequently, because of scheduling errors, important items are put last and are still being considered by some members as others leave the room, perhaps as members from another decision group meeting are waiting in the corridor. Both the chair and the members have a responsibility for seeing to it that the meeting starts and finishes on time. If you do not begin on time, you encourage people to be late. It is one of the paradoxes of the modern decision group that the courtesy we extend to latecomers, waiting to begin until they arrive, is the very act by which they define themselves as not being late. Lateness is determined not by the clock but by the meeting process itself. If the process has not begun, the person is not late. Without that understanding, problems of tardiness are unlikely to be changed. My answer, therefore, to the frequently asked question, "How can we get people to come on time?" is "Begin on time." We should follow the rule of that psychiatrist: Begin the meeting when it is supposed to begin and (even if that fails) end the meeting when it is supposed to end. A few episodes of this will convey the message to members that the meeting, in fact, will begin on time and end on time, and that this is an important factor in their deciding whether to attend.

There is a point at which the concepts of agenda integrity and temporal integrity fuse. Sometimes, certain decision group members cannot attend at a particular time or at a particular meeting. Most of us have busy schedules that make it impossible to attend every meeting. We therefore rely on the agenda, the "score" of the decision group orchestra, to tell us whether this is a performance that can be missed. My judgment is based on trust—trust that what is promised on the agenda will occur when it is supposed to occur. If you see on the agenda that the ABC report is not going to be considered till the latter half of the meeting, you can leave another meeting early to make the discussion. Imagine, then, that you find that the first meeting is late in starting and that they have not gotten to the ABC report at all nor are they likely to get to it. At that point, you feel like strangling members of the decision group, singly, and boiling them in oil, severally. Time wasting in cold blood and misallocation of time ought to be considered "misdemeanors," if not outright "felonies."

One way of protecting the integrity of agenda items is to schedule certain issues for discussion over a period of time; just as you can develop a meeting agenda, you can project agenda items over several meetings. I am referring to long-term scheduling. This simply means that by the year's end, those matters that are before the decision group for that year will have been dealt with. This requires

preplanning,

a system of allocating agenda items to future meeting dates, and

handling of assigned items at their scheduled time.

For this reason, agenda integrity and temporal integrity are closely linked. Typically, if agenda integrity is violated, temporal integrity is also violated, and the message that these two violations give to decision group members is that you are not going to seriously follow the schedule developed for the decision group activity over the year. Therefore, there is no great reason to put in the kind of effort that is needed to cover agenda items. At the end of the year, when you look back to assess your accomplishments, you will fund a stubble field of weeds, rocks, and only a few useful items scattered about.

Rules for Temporal Integrity
* Begin your meeting on time.
* End your meeting on time.
* Keep to the agenda and a rough time order for items.
* Develop, and keep, a long-range schedule.

ENSURING FOCUS: THE FRACTION RULES

Agenda and temporal integrity are supported by three "fraction rules":

The rule of halves
The rule of three quarters
The rule of thirds

The Rule of Halves. The rule of halves says that no item shall be entered on the agenda unless it has been given to the person who schedules the agenda items one half of the time between meetings. Thus, if it is a monthly meeting, the chair or the agenda scheduler must receive the item 2 weeks before the next meeting. It takes time to organize and prioritize items on an agenda. People coming to a meeting should know in advance what they will be discussing and what decisions may be expected of them. Some items require preparation, data gathering, and study in advance of the meeting.

The meeting planner sifts and sorts the items—sifting to see if the item is really a decision group item or whether some other disposition is appropriate and sorting to determine whether items are announcement-type items, decision or action items, or items for discussion and brainstorming. This determination is vital because these different items go on different places in the agenda.

If the planner does not have the items, it is impossible to get the right people and the right information to the meeting. It is also impossible to send the material out ahead of time (rule of three quarters, coming right up) because, of course, you do not have it!

How often have you found this rule violated? Material relevant to that discussion is passed out at the meeting, frequently in incomplete form. I'm certain you've experienced the panic of desperately skimming through the material while trying to participate in a discussion. Panic is not conducive to smooth performance. The equivalent process for an orchestra would be to pass out incomplete sections of the score as the orchestra members were walking in for the performance. More often than not, this kind of behavior sets the stage for panic and discord.

This approach to agenda building means that chairs and other meeting heads will not ask for "approval of the agenda." Why? First, all decision group members should have access to the agenda in advance. If somebody would like an item considered, it should be considered. The only thing required is that the chair be informed sufficiently early so that he or she can look over the items and get the necessary information required by the items.

The Rule of Three Quarters. The rule of three quarters is another checkpoint along the way to the meeting date. It requires that at the three-quarters point between meetings, the agenda be distributed along with any material required for effective preparation. In more formal meetings, this is typically called the "packet" and may involve an agenda and minutes of the previous meeting, followed by reports A, B, and C, to be discussed at the meeting. At less formal meetings, it is possible to incorporate some of the required material into the agenda.

Sending the agenda and accompanying items at the three-quarters point increases the likelihood that most participants will come to the decision group meeting adequately informed. For a monthly meeting, the rule of three quarters means that at the beginning of the third week, material has to be sent out. It also means that the chairs and people who make up decision groups can plan on a certain part of every month as a time when agenda items are coming in and when the final pulling together of material occurs prior to sending it out.

The Rule of Thirds. Generally, meetings fall into three psychological phases—a "get-go" phase, a "heavy work" stage, and a "decompression" stage—each about a third of the announced length of the meeting. Experience shows that important business should be handled as much as possible within the middle third of the meeting, which is when participants are likely to have most physical energy, the highest attendance, and the greatest psychological attention. Latecomers have arrived, early leavers will not yet have left. Items of lesser moment can be handled in the first third or the latter third of the meeting. Even if the meeting does start a little bit late, what one has to cut will not be as crucial.

The typical meeting is scheduled in the reverse of that order with items of ascending importance following one after the other until the last, and most crucial, item, which occurs close to the end of the meeting and before the usual category of new business. Because meetings typically begin late and run long, this means that the most important item is considered at the most pressured time. Undoubtedly, people will have already left. What we hoped would be balanced, reasoned discussion becomes hurried and frenetic, with only partial participation.

CONCLUSION

These five rules are essential to ensuring focus and aiding decision making in decision groups and boards:

1. *Agenda integrity:* All items on the agenda are discussed; no items not on the agenda are discussed.
2. *Temporal integrity:* Begin on time; end on time; and keep to a sensible internal schedule of items within the meeting.
3. *Rule of halves:* Get all items to be discussed to the agenda maker half the time between the meetings.
4. *Rule of thirds:* The agenda scheduler orders the items (he or she has them under the rule of halves) so that the most important items come in the middle third.
5. *Rule of three quarters:* After the rule of halves and the rule of thirds, give out the material; at the three-quarters point between meetings, all relevant material is sent to the members.

If applied, these will significantly improve the quality of the decision making of any decision group by strengthening the procedures that make for good decision making. Although good decision making does not automatically follow good procedures, it is a good deal less likely to occur without them. Decision making on complex issues cannot take place until there is a reasonable assurance that the procedures follow the proper order and permit the disciplined and reasonable application of intelligence to those items.

Now that she was chair of the Music Therapy Association, Bea Sharpe had the chance to correct some of the things she thought were wrong. She had worked with the group to develop a set of procedures that satisfied the Open Meetings Act for the State of Michigan, their home state. That success had brought her to the chairship. Meetings were at least beginning on time and ending close to on time. A social hour after the meeting seemed to be working well, and people looked forward to hearing a new piece, having some sherry, and visiting. They seemed to work harder during the meeting. She was beginning to be successful in getting agenda items early and making up an agenda. Things were looking up.

EXERCISE 3.1

RULES FOR MAINTAINING FOCUS

Pick a recent meeting that you have attended. Now that you have called it back to your mind, think about the five rules for maintaining focus. See if you can answer the following questions.

1. Was there agenda integrity? Were all scheduled items discussed? Were unscheduled items kept to a minimum? Was there an agenda in the first place?
2. Was there temporal integrity? Did the meeting begin and end on time?
3. Was the agenda set up so that the important information was available in advance (rule of halves)? Did it come out in time (rule of three quarters)?
4. Was the meeting run so that the most important items came in the middle third of the meeting (rule of thirds)?

Chapter 4

TEMPLATES FOR ACTION
The Agenda, the Minutes, and Reports

Hank left his fourth meeting of the day, of the Homeless Coordinating and Planning Council, feeling foul. As a local mental health executive, he had to attend more meetings and was on more decision groups and boards than anyone he knew. And the damn meetings were so unproductive. This last one in particular made his blood boil. No one had prepared anything, and everyone threw out different topics, problems, and solutions.

No one, it seemed, had taken the time to put things together. He had asked for an agenda. The chair had said, "Good. That's the first item, the agenda."

At that point, Hank had said, "Look, you folks. If you can't be better organized than this, I've got better things to do with my time." Then he left, while Bob Grey muttered something about "compulsive" types who want to stifle creativity.

As he went out the door, Hank thought, "That's not creativity; that's chaos."

Three documents have great potential for assisting the decision group in achieving high-quality results—the agenda, the minutes, and reports. That's the good news. On the downside, lack of attention to the actual physical structure of these three elements—how they are written, what they say, how they are configured—can create serious problems. Lack of an agenda or using the "stock agenda"—new business, old business, unbelievably old business, and so on—can provide fundamental distractions for the decision group. The minutes need to be nondistracting and configured so that they can provide the needed documentation for decision review. Reports need to be crafted so that they focus not on an item-by-item odyssey of what the subgroup did but create a crisp, clear focus on the items to be decided.

THE AGENDA

The agenda defines the purpose of a meeting. It relates that purpose—through the items on it—to the larger mission and the position of the organization. Available to the chair, group members, staffers, and executives, it is more than a list of topics. It is a substantive document that informs the members and other interested persons about how and when the decision group will make its decisions, the issues before the group, and the items that need thought (but not decision) for the future. Why, then, is the agenda so often glossed over? Typically, it is written a few minutes before the meeting, perhaps even at the meeting. Topics are listed with no regard for the information needed to consider the issues intelligently. This is, of course, not always the case. Topics listed in crude order are sometimes sent out in advance of the meeting, but all too frequently, these are not adequate to provide the guidance needed for preparation. In a word, they are not *functional.*

A TYPICAL MEETING

Before describing the frame of a functional agenda, I will look at the typical order of events at business meetings. I will then spell out what an agenda should be and can be. Along the way, I will suggest a set of rules that, if followed, will help shape and structure the meeting.

The Minutes and How They Are Discussed

The typical meeting begins with a review of the minutes of the previous meeting. Minutes summarize what occurred at that meeting. Properly written, they record all decisions made. If their accuracy is challenged, the review of the minutes not infrequently becomes the occasion for discussing last week's or last month's meeting all over again. This is especially true if the minute taker has attempted to present in depth what people said instead of what they decided. A tremendous amount of time is wasted on discussion of the minutes.

Reports: How They Are Made and Discussed

Many groups follow approval of the minutes with an extensive series of reports. One PTA meeting has 16 subdecision group reports always listed on the agenda, whether or not there is any report to be made. Unfortunately, finding their subdecision group listed forces subcommittee chairs to make some kind of a report—any kind. This is extremely time-consuming. People make reports even if they have nothing to say, and frequently, they will take the occasion to add something, which is then picked up by another individual and off the meeting goes. I recommend that the entire process of giving reports be stopped. This may seem extreme. It isn't.

Other Items

Many meetings are made up completely of discussions of the minutes and the reports. Sometimes there are other items, listed in random order or with the most difficult item saved till last. Meetings have a curious similarity to a therapy session, where the client will introduce trivial material during the major part of the hour, and only at the end, with just a few minutes remaining, share some important elements that really need discussion.

Why Does This Crazy-Making Occur?

I have already suggested some larger reasons why meetings go badly. We have no training. Participants fail to take the potential of meetings and the actuality of specific meetings seriously. These lead to the self-fulfilling prophecy: We think things will be bad and they will be, by gosh!

But there is another reason. Paradoxically, many decision groups actually seek to avoid decisions. A paradox is a seeming contradiction that can be understood by deeper reflection. In the case of decision groups (which are, really, almost all task forces, committees, boards, etc.), there is a fundamental tension between maintaining group cohesion on the one hand and taking action on the other. Decision making tears at the cohesion of the group. Because groups sense this, they seek to avoid decision, much the same as the client mentioned earlier uses trivial material to avoid getting to the serious material that really need surface.

Unfortunately, for both clients and groups, avoidance is not a good alternative. For groups, recognition of this tendency means that constant effort must be made to (a) keep groups focused on decisions to be made and (b) before the meeting comes to an end, repair the damage to cohesion that decisions create. The agenda structure, the minutes structure, and the reports structure, are each tailored to that end.

A NEW AGENDA STRUCTURE

I suggest eliminating the typical agenda of minutes, reports, old business, new business, and then miscellaneous business. What type of structure is an appropriate substitute? It is called the agenda bell (see Figure 4.1). In a bell curve agenda structure, easy decision items come before more difficult items. The most difficult decision item should appear in the

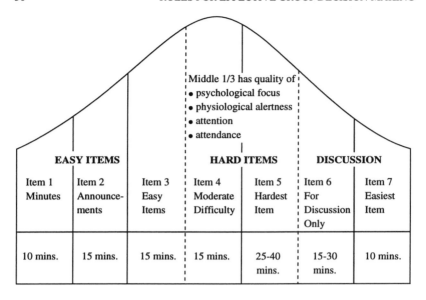

Figure 4.1. The Agenda Bell

middle. After that item has been dealt with (which is at about the two-thirds point of the meeting as the rule of two thirds, mentioned in the last chapter, suggested), there is a break, in the sense that there are no more decision items. Rather, the group moves on to items for discussion and brainstorming, where the generation of ideas is the key and openness is sought.

In the bell curve structure, I try to plan for seven types of items to be covered in a typical meeting.

Rules for Framing the Decision Group Meeting Agenda

1. Minutes
2. Announcements
3. (3a, 3b . . .) Short, easy items for decision or action
4. (4a, 4b . . .) Moderately tough items for decision or action
5. The most difficult item (only one)
6. (6a, 6b . . .) Items for discussion, brainstorming, and so on (nondecision items)
7. The least difficult item and adjournment

How does the agenda planner knows which items are which? Here is where the rule of halves links to the agenda. Because under the rule of halves the planner has received items in advance, he or she can go through the sorting process (mentioned in the last chapter) and allocate items to the appropriate categories.

Notice, too, that there are no reports as such in this agenda format. The old "report of the AIDS Awareness Committee" has now been replaced with an agenda item in one of the following categories: announcement (Category 2); decision—easy (Category 3), moderately tough (Category 4), tough (Category 5); or discussion (Category 6).

This agenda framework is quite different from the typical agenda framework that one sees. It requires preplanning and judgment on the part of the agenda maker. But it also requires keeping the faith with one's constituents. Members of the group must trust (and see) that the items they have suggested under the rule of halves are, in fact, there (or that members have been contacted earlier to receive an explanation of why their suggestion is not appearing as an agenda item).[1] It must be a vehicle for the group and never a partisan structure for the agenda planner.

1. Minutes

Minutes should be crisp and relatively brief, focusing on content and decisions that are explicitly linked to the agenda of the previous meeting. Follow this procedure and controversy over the minutes should be reduced, if not eliminated. Accuracy is all that should concern members. It is proper at this point to approve minutes or to correct inaccuracies. To keep members from using the minutes to rehash the last meeting's discussion, the chair should ask those who wish to discuss the minutes to suggest the "language they feel would be more appropriate." This focus on language tends to temper the tendency to use the minutes as a springboard for fresh discussion.

2. Announcements

Announcements are short, factual informative "bites" that are noncontroversial. This category is a flexible one that can be used to fill in some time if, in fact, the meeting had to begin with few people. It is essential that the meeting begin on time. Making announcements early before decisions have to be made respects those members who arrived on time and defines anyone who arrives afterward as late. Announcements are declarative, noncontroversial, and informative in nature. Discussion should be kept to a minimum. If an item provokes great discussion, then it should have been a regular agenda item and can be placed on the next meeting's agenda.

3. Short, Easy Items for Decision or Action

Less controversial or easier-to-handle decision items should appear early in the agenda, in order of increasing difficulty within this easy category. Thus 3a would be the easiest item, 3b the next easiest, and so on. Once the first decision has been made, participants feel freer, more confident that they can dispose of more difficult items.

4. Moderately Tough Items for Decision or Action

Category 3 items are then followed by items of a more difficult nature. Here, too, there is an ascending order of difficulty, from moderately tough (4a) to a bit tougher (4b), and so on.

Notice what I have done so far. The meeting has begun on time, and I have moved quite rapidly into a decision-making frame of mind. The very first activity led to a decision approval of the minutes. There was then a brief pause for announcements, followed by decisions or actions on several less difficult items.

By now, we should have completed approximately the first third of the meeting. The agenda has been written in such a way as to specify exactly what the decision desired is: approval of the minutes, appointment of the new executive director, and so on. People who read the agenda when they receive their packet know exactly what is asked of them. In this way, the agenda becomes a tool for structuring the meeting. It informs and shapes the behavior of members even in advance of their attendance.

5. The Most Difficult Item

At about the one-third point or a bit later, the agenda planner schedules the most difficult item. It occupies the middle section of the meeting. It is put there to take advantage of peak attendance. Latecomers will have arrived, and those making early departures will not yet have left. This location also capitalizes on psychological energy. It follows completed decisions that have made people feel good about their decision-making ability. Because they are not stuck at the end of the meeting, people will not have to consider key items as they are leaving the room. Giving ample time, usually 30 to 40 minutes (in a 2-hour meeting) for discussion of a difficult item increases the likelihood that it will be properly dealt with. If a decision is not reached in about 40 minutes, then additional work has to be done. Perhaps more information is needed. Perhaps the item should be tabled and brought back again. When that happens, it is perhaps unfortunate, but there may still be room to complete a bit more nondecision business. But the decision group has worked hard, and it is time for a break.

6. Items for Discussion, Brainstorming,
and So On (Nondecision Items)

Following the rule of thirds, we should be at the end of Item 5 approximately two thirds of the way through the meeting. Assuming that decisions have been made, the group needs a break during which possible harm to group cohesion can be repaired. This process occurs through the scheduling of nondecision items, "for discussion only" (FDO), and allows the members to continue to interact, look forward not back, and decompress as a group.

A brief stretch break sometimes helps. The chair might permit people to get up, walk around a little bit, shake themselves down. This not only provides physical relief but also defuses whatever animosities have been built up during the discussion of the difficult items that preceded the break. A 5-minute stretch can do a lot of good, but it may not be enough. The members have had a break. The meeting process needs to break as well.

FDO items help to release tensions. Members are informed in advance through its location on the agenda that no decision is going to be taken on this item or items. Having a time for FDO items does more. Too often, decisions are made prematurely, especially if there is a proposal for action before the group prior to adequate discussion.

When decision groups develop a habit of putting FDO items on the agenda, members look forward to discussions without decisions staring them in the face. FDO items provide an opportunity for the ventilation of feelings and the assessment of political orientations. It gives the chair, staffers, and group members an opportunity to survey the lay of the land. It sets the stage for compromises that can be made between meetings. The release of pressure at one meeting followed by opportunities for reassessment and for working out differences permits members to get down to business when the items come back on the agenda at the following meeting.

Two techniques of handling FDO items contribute to better decisions at the next meeting: (a) the "straw vote" technique and (b) the "in-principle" technique.

Straw Vote. Here, the chair, or a member, asks for preliminary indications on a straw vote basis of which series of discussed alternatives might be preferred. It helps organize discussion and helps staffers and subgroups to avoid wasting time in research on a particular issue or option that no one wanted anyway. This technique helps prioritize future activity.

In Principle. The in-principle technique, useful for other items as well, separates the "gut element"—the basic, fundamental, central feature—in a decision from lesser "how-to" aspects. For example, the Homeless Coordination and Planning Council might decide that, in principle, they would like to have a big fund-raising event in the spring. Details of the event will be discussed briefly but are not confused with the overall "principle" that a spring fund-raising event is a good idea. Once that in-principle decision is established or the in-principle orientation is known, it is possible to work out relevant options, avoiding matters of lesser interest. It also helps discussion to stick to the largest issue in principle or to details. Some discussions go from large principles to small details, and I call this "discussion oscillation." It is extremely difficult to participate in such a discussion because you are never sure at what level the issue is seen at any given moment.

7. The Least Difficult Item and Adjournment

It is always a good idea to end the meeting on a positive note, one of agreement and accomplishment. About 80% of the way through the meeting, the chair says that it is time to finish with a brief discussion of the last item or items—quickies that can be dispatched with ease. The psychological value of dispatching several items with ease is great, especially if the discussion up to that point has been difficult or outcomes problematic. This permits people to leave with a sense of orderliness, some sense of accomplishment. This is the point at which the meeting should be adjourned.

The end of this meeting is the beginning of the next meeting. Therefore, the psychological frame of mind, the social conditions of the meeting as it ends, for the person and for the group, are important determinants of whether someone will make the effort to come to the next meeting.

TIME

It is imperative that the agenda maker link the agenda structure to the clock so that one can cover the items in the time available. If it appears that there are too many items, then more meetings are necessary. The clock should be a "running clock," for example 1:00 to 1:10, so that people at the meeting can easily see whether they are keeping to the time schedule or not. Time blocks also signal the importance of items in a nonthreatening way.

WRITING THE AGENDA:
THE MEETING AS A RESTAURANT MENU

Now that the overall framework of the agenda has been established, the next thing is the problem of actually preparing the agenda document. The best model for an agenda that is really useful and helpful is taken from the structure of a restaurant menu, perhaps a fancy one. There, each "dish" is listed so that the reader can know exactly what he or she is ordering. As an additional helper, there is usually a sentence following the entreé listing that offers a bit more explanation. This model is a good entrée to follow. The example that follows brings these ideas together with the overall structure mentioned earlier.

HOMELESS PLANNING AND COORDINATING COUNCIL

Monthly Meeting
1:10-3:00 p.m.

The Salvation Army Conference Room
Celestial Blvd. Office

AGENDA

1:10-1:15	1. Approval of the minutes
1:15-1:20	2. Announcements
	Mental Health FAIR
	Thanksgiving preplanning
	Shelter wish list
1:20-1:30	3. Affiliation with Foodgatherers
	[ACTION]
	Membership Subcommittee proposes accepting Foodgatherers as council members
1:30-1:45	4. Request to the United Way
	[ACTION]
	Finance Committee recommends a supplemental request of $10,000
	[EXECUTIVE SUMMARY ATTACHED]
1:45-2:25	5. Strategic plan review
	[ACTION]
	The Strategic Planning Committee recommends approval of the new strategic plan (discussed once already as an Item 6)
	[EXECUTIVE SUMMARY ATTACHED]
2:25-2:50	6. Kellogg initiative
	[DISCUSSION]
	The Kellogg Foundation has written the Community Foundation about our community's becoming a test for the possibilities of reorganizing health care.
	[LETTER ATTACHED]
2:50-3:00	Thank-you note to the Jewish Federation
	Adjournment

MINUTES

Minutes, and how to take them, are a big problem in decision groups. Most of us use the "court reporter" process. By this, I mean minutes whose structure is very close to a verbatim record. Unfortunately, this style is very inefficient. It fails to highlight decisions and generates lots of discussion about corrections as people deny they said what they said. And to be frank, it is hard to record things "exactly." To help avoid stretching out the minutes into "hours," I suggest the focus be on content, not process.

Content minutes are an intelligent summary of the points of view expressed on a particular issue, without names attached. Review of the discussion is followed by the conclusion or decision made. The substance of the debate must be reflected, but every side comment, joke, and irrelevancy that crept into the discussion should be ruthlessly rooted out. Emphasize the key points—highlight them; don't hide them.

Decisions are listed in bold and boxed for attention. Here, names are named, places placed, dates mentioned.

The minutes should be "agenda-relevant" minutes. Agenda-relevant minutes are a form of content minutes in which the headings in the agenda are repeated in the minutes. With them, anyone can look at a copy of the agenda for the meeting of January 12, then at a copy of the minutes for January 12 and see topic identifications and find out what happened at the January 12 meeting. If a proposal from the ABC subgroup is discussed, the minutes explicitly identify the ABC report, record the discussion about it, and note the decision or action taken.

Who should take the minutes? Generally, the staff person assigned to the decision group takes them, or the duty is rotated from member to member. In the case of a board, if it is a "secretary," it is not necessary that that person be the one who always takes minutes. If this were so, the secretary would rarely be able to participate. Consider the secretary as the board or decision group archivist, the person who is responsible for keeping the records, for keeping a complete set of minutes, and, quite possibly, for issuing them after a rough draft has been received from the person who takes them.

Rules for Agenda-Relevant Minutes

- Report views without naming disputants.
- Summarize debate.

- **Record action taken.**

- Categorize items under agenda headings of the previous meeting.
- Assign recording to staffers or rotate recording among members.
- Share copies with key appropriate people, including anyone whose name appears in the record (see Exercise 4.1 at the end of this chapter).

Keep the following sample in mind.

HOMELESS PLANNING AND COORDINATING COUNCIL
MINUTES OF THE MONTHLY MEETING

Minutes

1. The minutes were approved as submitted.

2. Announcements

Mental Health FAIR

There will be a mental health fair at the armory next Friday, all day. Extend invitations broadly and come and help out if you can.

Thanksgiving preplanning

The Holiday Coalition is meeting next month to contact food and shelter sources for upcoming holidays. If you have any ideas, call Matt Tropman @ 313-663-3411.

Shelter wish list

The shelter, as usual, needs linens, towels, lightbulbs, and two padlocks. If you have any of these please contact the shelter.

3. Affiliation with Foodgatherers

The membership of Foodgatherers was discussed. Appreciation was expressed for their excellent work.

> **The proposal to have Foodgatherers as a constituent member was approved.**

4. Request to the United Way

Discussion of the UW supplemental raised the issue of whether or not this submission would possibly harm future funding. After a call to the United Way CPO, it was determined that it was completely independent of future funding requests.

> **The Proposal to submit the supplemental request was approved. Sid Schoen will take care of the final details, see that it is sent in, and provide copies for others on the council.**

5. Strategic plan review

Considerable time was spent reviewing the proposed strategic plan for the homeless. (Version 3 was the one on the table.) The plan was made up of vision, mission, and strategic suggestions for the coming year. The vision and mission were warmly received; however, there was some difference of opinion with respect to the mix (or weighting) of the elements in the annual plan. Differences occurred over whether to put 80% of the council's energy on direct service to the homeless or whether to reduce that amount and spend more time on coordination.

> **It was decided to approve the vision and mission portions of the plan and approve the annual plan with the following emendations: 50% of the council's time shall be spent in direct service to the homeless; 50% shall be spent in efforts at coordination. Ty-Ur Flies will send out fresh copies to council and to relevant agencies. Jim-Bob Clancy will prepare press releases and follow up with other media.**

6. Kellogg initiative

Guest: Hugo First, President of the Community Foundation

Seymour Smity, the Kellogg Foundation

The Kellogg Foundation has written the Community Foundation about our community's becoming a test for the possibilities of reorganizing health care. There was much discussion about the proposed suggestion and what it might mean. Members felt that a considerable challenge would be expressed through the need for coordination, collaboration, and networking of all organizations. Concern was expressed about whether the community was really ready for a community-level effort of this magnitude. Several members pointed out that such an undertaking would require organizations to take a community benefit view as well as an "organizational benefit" view. Nonetheless, there was enthusiasm expressed by the group, and the Community Foundation and the Kellogg Foundation both offered encouragement.

It was agreed to have a further discussion of this important topic at the next meeting. It was also agreed that some representatives from the local hospitals and health care organizations should be invited to sit in. Edsel Over agreed to make those contacts.

6. Thank-you note to the Jewish Federation

A thank-you note was sent to the Jewish Federation for arranging for volunteers during the Christmas Day food bank.

Adjournment @3! Thank you all.

John Penman, Executive Director, Homeless No More

REPORTS

Reports are another problem in decision groups. Often, subgroup chairs do not know how to prepare them or what to ask of the group to which they are reporting. If the chair checks with subdecision group chairs sometime before the halfway point between meetings, it should not be difficult to find out if there is something to report and, if so, what. If there is nothing to report, the group is simply not scheduled on the agenda. Only those items requiring action or providing other decision groups with information that can help them out should be listed on the agenda. They should be listed in such a way as to communicate to the reader the problems the subgroups have been working on, options for dealing with the problems, and actions invited or recommended.

Instead of listing "the ABC report" on the agenda, include notes with each item that suggests that action should be taken, as I mentioned in the discussion of agenda construction: for example, "Consideration of the ABC report," "Approval of school bus purchase," "Ratification of the budget," "Hiring of the new executive," and so on. Communicating the invited action in the language of the agenda will go a long way toward informing members in advance of the meeting what they being asked to do. It is also likely to encourage them to read decision group reports before the meeting. That's where they belong—before, not during, the meeting.

Reports given verbally are one of the greatest time wasters with which decision groups must cope. If there is no action coming from the report, a summary report, in writing, can be attached as an appendix to the minutes and agenda that go out in the member's packet. It is much easier to scan a paragraph than to listen to a paragraph. Oral paragraphs tend to expand and expand. Shaving the agenda down to action items communicates an action-oriented message to the membership. The rule of halves, you will recall, specifies that the chair or staffer call subdecision group people to inquire about their reports. If one meets monthly, then a call toward the beginning of the second week not only secures information but prods the individual to "get cracking." There should be sufficient time between the call and the meeting to handle problems. But if they cannot be handled, the report may focus on the problem itself, which then becomes an item of business.

THE EXECUTIVE SUMMARY

It is better that the scheduled reports not be sent out in their entirety. Perhaps the greatest single complaint from members, staffers, and chairs about the decision group and board process is about volumes of paper produced and not read. Part of the reason that people do not read reports is that they have only a 50% likelihood of being discussed at the meeting. A contributing reason, however, may be found in the bulk of the report itself. This is why I feel it is much better to prepare an "executive summary" of long and detailed reports. This

limits material to a one- or two-page digest,

highlights key issues, and

links material to major report by reference notes.

Good executive summaries need not be longer than 10% of the original document. If effectively written, they may stimulate members to ask for the full report. A report requested by a member is likely to be read more carefully. What should go out with the agenda, then, is not a thick wad of reports but a thin packet of executive summaries. People who are pressed for time and who never read a full report often glance fairly systematically at the executive summary.

THE OPTIONS MEMO TECHNIQUE

An excellent way to prepare the executive summary is in "options memo form." Options analysis involves considering the alternatives available to the decision group, given present information, and presenting them in an order that promotes decision group discussion. These are put in writing.

When that is done, the staffer can and should add his or her own recommendations (as long as these are clearly distinguished from the options).

Rules for an Options Memo

- Analyze the problem.
- Present alternative solutions.
- Offer staffer and subgroup recommendations (see Exercise 4.2 at the end of this chapter).

The bulk of the discussion is focused on the preliminary recommendations. The decision group essentially looks for four kinds of elements in the preliminary recommendation, using the following analysis template.

Analysis Template

1. Is the logic that drove the selection of one option over the others presented persuasively?
2. Is the judgment persuasive?
3. Do any hidden problems remain in the preliminary recommendation that were missed by the subgroup looking at the issue?
4. Are there ways that the preliminary recommendation can be improved?

When all four items have been positively addressed, the preliminary recommendation (as emended through Action 4) can become a final recommendation or decision.

Rules for Handling Reports

- List only relevant action and discussion elements of reports.
- Note expected activity.
- Summarize reports requiring no action.
- Send executive summaries of scheduled reports.
- Use the options memo technique for presentation.
- Use the four-point analysis template.

CONCLUSION

Proper attention to the agenda and its use as a central tool for decision group accomplishment will greatly enhance decision group accomplishment. It is one of the simplest, most direct ways to begin a process of improved decision group decision making. For this to happen, however, the agenda maker must recognize that the agenda is a complex document that requires proper observance of structure, proper awareness of the form of minutes, proper concern for the nature of reports, and proper regard for the very language in which the agenda is written. If all of these things occur, the agenda can become a vital tool for effective meetings. Remember, rather than using the traditional, or at least usual, agenda (beginning with reports and having the key business left, often, until last), place the most important matters in the middle of the meeting so that they can be completed by approximately the two-thirds point in the meeting. That will be a great help.

> After Hank left, the meeting of the Homeless Coordinating and Planning Council group petered out.
>
> Bob Grey had been angry with Hank. "Who does he think he is, anyway?" Bob said to the group. "Everyone knows that it is important to have freedom from constraints."
>
> Bob had been the chair and secretly felt chagrined at Hank's outburst. Not only was it something, he felt, of a personal criticism, but Hank was an influential man in town and personally respected. He controlled important budget allocations as well.
>
> At that point, Peter Josephs spoke up. "Maybe Hank did have something of a point," he said. "Why don't we have a meeting and talk about our meetings."
>
> "Good," said Fran Fox. "But let's each send Bob a little note about what could be better first. Then he can see what suggestions and problems we have in common and make a sort of list."
>
> "Fine," Peter said. "And I'll call Hank and see if we can get him back on the track." People left feeling much better about their activity than they had over the past year.

NOTE

1. There can be many reasons for an item's not being included on the agenda: There was not enough time; more information was needed; it turns out to be a one-on-one type item; and so on. But these reasons are fully "processed" with the person who suggested the item.

EXERCISE 4.1

MINUTES

Consider the rules for agenda-relevant minutes. Does a group you select follow these rules for the minutes of its meetings?

- Report views without naming disputants.
- Summarize debate.

• **Record action taken in a box.**

- Categorize items under agenda headings of the previous meeting.
- Assign recording to staffers or rotate recording among members.
- Share copies with key appropriate people, including anyone whose name appears in the record.
- If not, consider ways that the minutes could be improved.

EXERCISE 4.2

RULES FOR AN OPTIONS MEMO

Consider this sample memo:

Memo to: Bea Sharpe, Chair, Compensation Committee

Memo from: Sally Swingle, Staffer

Re: Policy options for Salary Increments

You asked me to consider what a raise policy might be. Various staffers have different views on what would be appropriate. I have talked with them, and I have also looked at other agencies and identified the following options:

1. An across-the-board increase in dollars (this gives people differential percentage increases)
2. An across-the-board increase in percentages (this gives people differential dollar increments)
3. Some mix (note that dollar increases benefit those earning lower salaries; percentage increases benefit those earning higher salaries)

In addition, there are various bases on which any of the three principles might be used:

a. Merit, in which some measure of ability/contribution is used
b. Seniority, in which some measure of organizational age is used

My personal recommendation is to use a 1 and a. I would be happy to discuss this with the committee at its convenience.

cc. committee members

Now, think of some recent situation in which you had a report. See if that information can be boiled down to a memo as compact as this one. Note the three parts: analysis, options (1-3; a, b), and recommendation.

Chapter 5

ACHIEVING AN EFFECTIVE MEETING
Mechanics Of Decision Group Process

> Bill DeForrest was doing a lot of thinking as he walked toward the weekly staff meeting of Foodgatherers. He had had some criticism from his staff about the way meetings were run. He viewed it as a time of sharing—when everyone could get together and let each other know what was happening. But the staff had felt it was something of a waste of time. So he had developed a charter for the group, outlining the things that the group should be doing, and they had helped in that. He had begun to use agendas. One of his student interns was from the University of Michigan, and he had told Bill about a system for making agendas that he had learned about in administration class. It actually had worked very well. But there were still problems. The group never seemed to come to any conclusions on anything. Some participated, but some did not. Now *he* felt frustrated, and some of the staff did too.

Despite lots of preparation, things can still go poorly at decision group meetings. This can happen for many reasons. But perhaps the most important is what might be called "decision avoidance psychosis." There are lots of examples of this illness in groups.

MAJOR EXAMPLES OF
DECISION AVOIDANCE PSYCHOSIS

When organizations put off making decisions that need to be made until the very last minute (or even after the last minute), that's decision avoidance psychosis. One example of this illness is the "nondecision"—a decision appears to have been made, but actually, it has not been. Things go along very much as they have. Over time, this pattern of nondecision can lead to the "boiled-frog phenomenon." In an experiment described by Tichy and Devanna (1986), a frog is put in a petri dish filled with water, and the water is slowly heated over a burner. The frog boils to death. Why does it not leave? The answer seems to be that the just noticeable difference in the temperature is never enough to cause action. This just-noticeable-difference phenomenon is an important source of nondecision in organizations. Members see things pretty much as they were, and thus there is no need to act.

A second example is decision randomness. This process was outlined in the work already mentioned, Cohen et al.'s (1972) famous paper, "A Garbage Can Model of Organizational Choice." They argue that organizations have four roles or vectors within them: (a) problem knowers (people who know the difficulties the organization faces), (b) solution providers (people who can provide solutions but do not know the problems), (c) resource controllers (people who don't know problems and don't have solutions but control the allocation of people and money in the organization), and (d) a group of decision makers looking for work (or decision opportunities). They argue that for effective decision making, all these elements must be in the same room at the same time. In reality, most organizations combine them at random, as if tossing them into a garbage can. No wonder bad decisions result.

Decision drift, or "the Abilene paradox," is another famous "bad-decision" case (Harvey, 1974). In this case, a group of people were outside of Abilene, Texas, with nothing to do. It was hot. Somehow, they went into town (many miles, dusty drive, no air-conditioning) to have a very bad meal. On the way back, the "search for guilty parties" began. The Abilene paradox is used to identify those situations in which there never really was a decision to take a particular action. It is, as readers will recognize, very common.

Decision coercion, or groupthink, is another very well known decision problem (Janis, 1983). It is a false agreement in the face of power. One kind of power is group cohesion. In very cohesive groups, there is a strong wish to maintain the cohesion of the group. This commitment to the group sometimes means that alternatives are not really explored and options are not really considered, because such processes might cause differences within the group, potentially harming cohesion. This situation is very common in the human service community. A second kind of groupthink power involves an intimidating executive. When such a boss says, "We're all agreed then," most at the table say, "Aye." Only later, in the hallway, when the *real* discussion occurs, do the problems surface.

The reason for these problems is at least twofold. One part of it is that decision groups often do not know where they are unless someone vocalizes an action—actually says, "Let's try option X." A second reason is that actually proposing something in groups, especially cohesive groups, is scary, because your proposal might be rejected.

What is missing here, and what can be very helpful in the meeting itself, is the process of decision crystallization.

THE PROCESS OF
DECISION CRYSTALLIZATION

Many times in groups, as discussion is progressing, someone will say, "Well, where are we?" Often, that question is an invitation for someone, usually someone *else,* to sum up and propose a conclusion to the current discussion. Frequently, no one answers that question, and the discussion drags on and on. This is a situation in which the Abilene paradox can occur, in which "boiled frogism" begins, and other problems of decision avoidance occur.

It turns out that the key for decision groups is for there to be *vocalization* of an alternative. That is because many times a group does not know what it thinks until it hears it spoken out loud. Of course, that often means that the group does not like what it hears and may express disagreement with the vocalizer. Vocalizers often take the disagreement personally—and perhaps they should, because most of us do not vocalize except for those things that we really want; thus rejection is, in a way, personal. Vocalization here, however, is actually *on behalf of the group, not because it is your own preference.*

Generally, vocalization should occur after a round of discussion. A round of discussion is that point in a meeting—and we all recognize them—when there is a lull, when everyone has said one thing or those who wish to have said one thing. Here is a key point in the flow of decision process.

If, at that point, a member or a chair takes leadership by *summarizing what has been said so far and, then, suggesting a logical action that flows from that summary,* groups are grateful. It is often the case that first vocalization is not the final decision; actually it should not be. Decisions, in a way, are built through a process of

vocalization→improvement→vocalization→improvement, etc.

As members of the decision group hear the initial vocalization, they suggest improvements that could make the proposal better; then the group thinks that over and adds more improvements. And so the process goes. It is a dynamic interaction between ideas and improvements. Throughout, there is blending of people and ideas.

It is important to remember that the vocalizer should act on behalf of the group and avoid reacting emotionally when group members indicate disagreement. Not only will the decision avoidance problems be avoided, but the group will be well on the way to making high-quality decisions.

Recognizing when a round of discussion has been completed is something of an art, but most of us will have no trouble with it now that we know to look for it. Furthermore, it is alright to take leadership here. We do not have to wait for the chair or others to take leadership. We can take it—and we should take it.

OTHER ISSUES IN
MEETING MANAGEMENT

Managing the transition to decision is not the only thing that must be managed in a meeting. It is perhaps the key thing, because, after all, decisions are the product of the group. There are also issues of attendance, refreshments, participation, and special types of meetings, such as the first meeting. These are the most common difficulties encountered by decision groups. They come up repeatedly. I'll take them one at a time.

Attendance. How do we get people to attend meetings? To find an answer, we might do well to ask another question: Why don't people attend in the first place? As mentioned earlier, all too often the answers suggest some peculiarity of the offender's personality. Although this may occasionally be true, in the majority of cases, a look at decision group minutes, agenda, and modus operandi makes it clear why people do not attend. Procedures are sloppy, agendas are indistinct, and there is no harmony of process and no apparent order. Meetings seem to begin and end at will. Thus, when a member, particularly a thoughtful member, has to evaluate his or her time against the disappointing experience of the meeting itself, the meeting loses.

So let's begin with the decision group structure itself. I have made several suggestions, many of a tidying-up nature, that can make decision group work more orderly and that emphasize keeping to declared goals. These suggestions included trimming down reports, shaping and focusing discussion items, and using the bell curve structure. These kinds of changes streamline and rationalize the decision group process. They often do wonders for the attendance. People begin to say, "Well, things are really getting done now. It's worth coming to this meeting."

Sometimes, it is important to look at the system of announcing a meeting and reminding people of the meeting date and time. A two-media method of communication might include one contact by letter and another by phone. A written announcement might include a returnable card. I have found that the use of two reminders rather than one, each conveyed by different media, results in a clearer message and better attendance.

Still, if even after all these efforts, some still do not attend, it is time to look at the problems facing individual members. Sometimes people are just too busy to attend.

One approach is to secure the input of the missing person even though he or she cannot attend. It is called *remote participation*. One of the virtues of having the agenda so detailed is that people can tell the chair or another member what their views are, and these can be conveyed to the meeting. It can also be conveyed through a memo. It's not the best way to participate, but it is better than nothing, if it is occasional.

Finally, of course, you can explore with the member whether he or she is overcommitted. If that is the case, then you can offer to switch the member to an *ex officio* membership, a consultancy, or some other role that takes advantage of the member's contribution but does not demand regular attendance.

Rules for Correcting Nonattendance

- Streamline the procedures.
- Use two-media communication to remind members about attendance.
- Encourage remote participation when needed.
- Find out if a member is over committed and arrange for a different form of participation.

Food. What about food at meetings? A good rule of thumb is the following: The less food *during* meetings, the better. Food is convivial, inclusive. It is great before the meeting or, even better, after the meeting. Having food available during a meeting is distracting: Somebody crunches on the celery or knocks over the milk reaching for a second helping of spaghetti, a plate slips onto someone's budget report, and so on. The meeting process is interrupted with "Pass the salt, please," "Delicious prime rib," or "Can I have a second helping" Food diverts a meeting. But people need to be fed, and we all like a reward. Thus, as a meeting planner, you can turn food into a reward for good decision group performance, not into an agenda item. Nothing is as pleasant as a good meal after a heavy morning's work. Coffee, however, is permissible, but take care about who makes the coffee and who pays for the coffee. Trivial as those items seem, they become sufficiently large to block decision group progress simply by taking up time. Refreshments available at the break, on the other hand, are welcome.

Rules of Thumb About Food

- Discourage food during the meeting, but allow coffee.

- Provide refreshments at break time.
- Use food as a prereward or a reward, available only before or after, never during the meeting.

The First Meeting. Perhaps no meeting is more important than the first meeting. We all know that first impressions of a class, a professor, a potential date, or a business partner have a lasting effect. The first meeting, too, is absolutely crucial in setting the mood and pace of the particular decision group. If the chair strolls in late and without apparent thought to the meeting beforehand, this conveys a lack of seriousness that is immediately picked up by the decision group. Regardless of whether that impression is correct, it will stick. Getting a bad reputation is easier than shedding it.

For this reason, lots of attention should be paid to all aspects of the first meeting, whether it is the decision group's, the chair's, or the staffer's first meeting. Investment there will pay dividends later in quicker work and a smoother process. In particular, it is useful for the chair to take the opportunity to call each member of the decision group to talk with him or her, however briefly (but privately), about his or her hopes, personal agenda for the decision group, and potential areas of interest and contribution. Apart from being courteous, this discussion is an essential part of the chairperson's intelligence-gathering procedures. It provides a clear picture of a decision group's potential competency, interests, and orientation.

Rules for the First Meeting

- Contact members beforehand about their concerns.
- Be prepared with an agenda.
- Be on time.
- Set the model for future meetings.

Participation Control. How about the member who talks too much? There are a lot of Tommy Talkalots in the world, yet we encourage them with vague agendas and by failing to be clear about the topic of discussion. Chairs and members need to enforce rules of relevance, a task made easier with a more detailed agenda. It is impossible, however, to enforce such rules without topical focus. If, for example, the topic up for discussion is the budget, then little can be introduced that does not relate to that massive topic. The member's position is crucial here. It is not just the chair's job. Sometimes, members sit back and let the chair do all the work, secretly delighted that Tommy is "really giving it to the chair this time."

Obviously, then, participation can be focused by having more specific agenda items, through greater and better targeting of topics for discussion.

Then, for example, the chair can ask Tommy Talkalot whether his point is for or against the item up for discussion. That kind of intervention on the chair's part is legitimate, however, only if that is clearly the activity required. Beyond that, I encourage chairs to call on the less vocal members before calling on the talkative member. It is sometimes necessary, as everyone knows, to ask such a member to wait until others have had their turn or to remind that person that he or she has already had a turn and others now need to take theirs. Generally speaking, the decision group will support chair intervention if the chair is evenhanded and if it appears that this prerogative is not being used to simply silence views that are "out of synch" with the chair's. The quiet member, of course, should be drawn out as much as the talkative member's output should be tempered. Frequently, direct questions about the quiet member's opinion on this or that are helpful. Sometimes, the chair or another member can take the opportunity to meet with a quiet member outside of the meeting, discern his or her views and then ask whether or not to report the quiet member's views if the member him or herself does not wish to do so. Sometimes, people are waiting to be asked. This kind of invitation is enough to get them rolling. Sometimes, they are confused about matters but are embarrassed to say so. Great sensitivity is needed to find out why people are quiet. The different reasons one uncovers for this situation can lead to radically different modes of intervention.

Rules for Better Participation

- Emphasize the issue on agenda.
- Focus on decisions to be reached or items to be clarified.
- Target the discussion.
- Orchestrate comments.
- Draw out silent members.
- Temper overbearing members' output (see Exercise 5.1 at the end of this chapter).

CONCLUSION

There are many situations in which groups avoid making decisions or make poor decisions. In fact, the "poor decision" is so well understood as an output of group activity that there are names for several specific types —group think, the Abilene paradox, and the boiled frog—being among them. The problem is that the "antidote" to these poisonous processes—the technique of decision building—is not well understood. Decision building involves working back and forth among a vocalizer and the group members with the vocalizer articulating possibilities; keeping the parts of those possibilities where agreement is present; adding, changing, revocalizing improved alternatives; and so on over (sometimes) several iterations. The vocalizer works *on behalf of the group*. It can make all the difference.

On his way home from a recent meeting, Bill DeForrest allowed himself to enjoy a glow of satisfaction. He thought that he should actually pay that intern. Not only had the suggestion for agenda construction worked well, but the student had told him about the process of "decision crystallization," where one tries to construct a decision through a kind of back-and-forth interaction between himself and the staff group. At first it had been a bit awkward, but soon he got the hang of it, and the staff did too. It was working so well that several staff had written him a note of congratulations on the "new" staff meetings. "Life may get better than this" he thought, "but not by much."

EXERCISE 5.1

ACHIEVING PARTICIPATION

Select a recent meeting. Look at it from the perspective suggested in this chapter. In particular, let's consider participation. Did the meeting allow the chair and members to do the following:

- Emphasize the issue on agenda.
- Focus on decisions to be reached or items to be clarified.
- Target the discussion.
- Orchestrate comments.
- Draw out silent members.
- Temper overbearing members' output.

Why or why not? How could it be better?

PART II

Positions and Roles for Effective Group Decision Making

Decision group meetings are like orchestra performances in other ways. Orchestras have a lot of rehearsal; players have gone over their parts individually, in small groups (to play particularly difficult sections), and they have, of course, been rehearsed by the conductor. Each of the musicians knows his or her position, as does the conductor.

Although the decision group does not perform a concert, it does perform the act of decision making. The chair of a decision group is like the conductor of an orchestra, and when one becomes a conductor, one gives up instrumental virtuosity. The audience does not expect the conductor to conduct for a while, then jump down into the orchestra pit and into the oboe section, do a little run on the oboe, jump back through the violin section, fiddle around there a bit, hit the piano on the way out, and continue to conduct. Nor does the orchestra expect the timpanist to run up from the drums, do a little conducting, then run back, boom out a few booms on the drum, then run back to do a little more conducting.

Yet our decision group meetings are often just like that—sometimes with four or five conductors conducting at the same time from the same podium (with different pieces of music in mind), the musicians reading from different or incomplete scores so that none of them are together, with conductors running down from the podium into the orchestra, playing instruments. In fact, if we saw an orchestra perform the way many of our decision groups do, we would walk out. Yet we do not apply to those decision groups the same kind of rules that we would apply to an orchestra and expect an orchestra to follow. The key thing is that everyone has a position to play. When you change your position, you change your position. That has to be understood as we move about the decision group orchestra.

Four positions will be discussed in this section—chair, member, executive, and staffer. These are *positions* because one can be appointed to them. They have formal status within the group, with a set of expectations surrounding each position, even though this expectation set is quite varied. Indeed, it is so varied that when we accept a position as a chair, a member, a staffer, or an executive, we ourselves are not sure what we expect, not to mention what others might expect. This section provides some clarification of these points.

There is also a chapter on roles. Positions should be distinguished carefully from *roles*. Roles are informal and self-appointed (although there may be some exceptions to the self-appointment norm as people are asked to play a certain role in a meeting.) They are usually of short duration, as, for example, *the role of leader*. This role is something one must take on. One can be appointed chair or member but not leader. Similarly, there is the role of *follower*. Followers are needed if leaders are to work. There are the famous *task and process roles*. One could add *devil's advocate* and the less well-known *angel's advocate*. There are also *intellectual and interpersonal roles*.

A couple of generalizations are important to remember. First, over time, the people in each position should demonstrate all the roles. A chair is both a leader and a follower. Second, for this reason, one should seek to develop a role repertoire—a familiarity with the different roles and an ability to play them as needed.

Chapter 6

THE CHAIR

The phone rang and Marcia Waggoneer found herself talking to her old friend, Armondo Gloxman. "Marcia," Armondo said, "the nominating committee of the board would like to put your name in as chairperson for the coming year. We hope you will agree."

"Chair!" Marcia thought. "I have been interested—but I really have no idea what I am supposed to do as chair."

"Armondo," she asked, "What does the committee have in mind for the tasks and responsibility of a chair?"

"Oh, it's not much," Armondo replied. "Just show up at meetings with your whip, chair, and leather boots, and keep the group in line. It's a breeze."

Most of think that the chair is a kind of lion tamer and the members are rapacious lions. Those chairs who do not keep order are sometimes consumed *on* the job before being consumed *by* the job. We assume that the chair is responsible for what happens, or does not happen, in the decision group. But that assumption ignores the member's importance and position in the decision group. The chair suffers the "perils of headship" because he or she is the front-runner, the lead dog, the point person in the assignment of responsibilities. Certainly, just as the conductor of an orchestra has a crucial position to play, so does the chair of a decision group. The chair has a wide range of decisions to make and procedures to establish that influence the course of decision group activity. But the chair is not solely responsible for these decisions and actions. Every orchestra conductor needs the orchestra. But there are some important considerations that chairs-to-be might want to review, even if only in one's own mind, before accepting the position. It is also true that one cannot always choose these acceptances. Still, a little forethought goes a long way.

Prethinking about the task at hand is an important first step. But suppose one accepts. What then? What are chairs actually supposed to do?

CONSIDERATIONS FOR A CHAIR-TO-BE

The following discussion provides checkpoints to consider before accepting a chairship. In looking at what a candidate for the chair or a candidate for membership on a board or decision group must consider, let us focus on the following considerations.

Touchstones for Decisions About Acceptance
- Know the conditions for acceptance.
- Clarify the meaning of membership.
- Be clear about the group's mandate.
- Clarify the meaning of acceptance (see Exercise 6.1 at the end of this chapter).
- Ask for specific resources.

Conditions of Acceptance. An initial issue to explore is the conditions surrounding the job. Are the conditions that accompany a chairship inviting? One of the perversities of decision group life is that our friends and colleagues encourage us to take positions without the authority or resources to back them up. We then get blamed when we cannot do the job. This is why chair candidates should, if possible, specify the conditions under which they will accept the position. Such conditions for the chair may include the following:

The meaning of membership
The mandate
Transition to a different position in the group
Specification of resources
Specification of staff assistance
Specification of certain kinds of membership

If agreement on these items cannot be made at the start, further work on the decision group will probably be frustrating, if not pointless.

These suggestions represent a large order, and many of us will not be able to follow them all of the time. Too, there are decision groups and boards, such as community action groups, with which things have run poorly in the past. It is a challenge to get these groups back on track. The key principle is to think ahead. One should always keep this principle in mind if the others cannot be used or the conditions are not right for them. Think ahead about the decision group or board—your reasons for being on it (one set of thoughts) and the reasons others have for wanting you to be on it (another set of thoughts). If you can keep these two perspectives in mind—what you think and what others might think—it will help place your membership in perspective.

The Meaning of Membership. Those who appoint chairs and invite certain members to join a decision group are aware of the symbolic meaning of that invitation. Therefore, it is important for both chair and member to know how the public perceives their positions and their appointment to those positions. For example, a woman who will be perceived as a token member must be told that this is how the public will see her, even if this information is distasteful to her and even if she sees her role differently. That kind of knowledge enhances position performance and clarifies actions toward the member in question that might otherwise be quite puzzling.

This type of personal analysis is extremely hard because it frequently involves seeing ourselves unpleasantly as others see us. For this reason, it is a good idea for chairs to have a mentor, an individual in whom they trust, whose judgment they believe is objective and capable, to whom they can turn in situations of uncertainty and say, "What do you think? What does this mean?" All too often, we leave chairs twisting slowly in the wind, unsure of their position and what is expected of them. When they fail to perform, we blame them for poor performance.

The Mandate. All decision groups should have a written copy of their mandate, which is the statement of mission and position. Prospective chairs and members should have access to it. Unfortunately, these are not always available, especially if the decision group is new. I strongly urge that the would-be chair get a statement in writing from the appointing authority. If this cannot be provided, the chair candidate can write to the authority after their meeting and say something such as, "This is my understanding of what we discussed. Is it correct? Do you have any changes?" If no changes are made, that will do as a statement of mandate.

Doing this not only guides the chair and the membership in assessing whether the job is worthwhile, but it also enables the chair to provide copies of such a statement to members. If there is no statement of mandate to an already-established decision group, it should be possible to abstract one from various materials, such as annual reports or previous minutes.

This mission statement becomes the basis on which a decision group forms operational goals at the end of its period and assesses its performance. Typically, mandates or mission statements are quite broad, and the decision group will need to specify, in operational terms, how it wishes to go about the tasks it is asked to do. This often becomes the annual, semiannual, or monthly process in which goals are identified. These guide a decision group in its work and provide an overall schedule of agenda items. Agendas are shaped by the will of the members and guided by the long-term mandate, mission, and position of the decision group. They are also guided by the time frame required to enhance and ensure goal accomplishment.

The chair-to-be can add points to the mission statement during the "request" period while the acceptance is pending. It is a negotiating point. Some of the things a chair-to-be might wish to specify could involve limitations and focus of a mandate or limiting or expanding decision group responsibilities in certain areas.

Position Acceptance and Transition. Transition in position from member to chair can require major shifts in orientation and an acceptance of the constraints and responsibilities of the new position. For the chair, position acceptance means a shift from primary concern with one's own agenda to central responsibility for the agenda of the group as a whole. This point trips up many chairs, who sometimes use their position to grant and receive favors to advance their own fairly narrow interests.

To understand how inappropriate this is, it may help to refer again to the orchestra analogy. When the chair leaves the position of virtuoso candidate and becomes conductor of the decision group orchestra, he or she assumes a new position. Chairs, like conductors, are not evaluated on the basis of whether they can make some individually brilliant contribution; rather, their evaluation comes from weighing the orchestra's (or decision group's) performance under their guidance. Movement in the other direction can be just as difficult. It is best that a person not serve for a year on a group that she or he has just finished chairing. The position transitions can be too complex. Even if the individual can manage it, others within the group may find the transition difficult.

Because it is the statesperson's position that gives the chair added authority, the chair must cultivate that position and also handle it with some care. If it appears to the decision group that the chair is using the position to further narrow personal interests, then special privileges should be withdrawn. This process is a subtle one—no horns blare, no announcement is made. The symptom is that people are less willing to follow the chair's lead. Business seems to take longer, and more evidence and proof is requested. Should the chair ask about the situation in any specific instance, he or she is likely to be assured that all is well and that there just was a feeling that, in this particular instance, more was needed. This reassurance belies the facts. People no longer trust the chair.

Specification of Resources. As a part of the acceptance process, the chair-to-be might want to ask for certain resources with which to do the job the decision group is asked to complete. Sometimes, such resources take the form of staff assistance or the addition of certain kinds of membership. As part of the process of such "political" analysis, chairs and members should periodically review the decision group membership. The chair should examine the list of members to see who is in the group, what they want, what their interests are, and what topics they will probably push. Members should be sensitive to the position and orientation of the chair and other members because these orientations tend to shape the emerging structure of the decision group. Essentially, I am suggesting the development of an "intelligence system" to generate information about the persuasions and preferences of the membership. Having "no idea that Sam P. felt this way" indicates that proper homework was not done. (Recall from the earlier discussion on membership that it is mission driven, so that if the mission is changed or refocused, some adjustment of membership might be needed.)

RESPONSIBILITIES OF THE CHAIR

In addition to these rather specialized positions or roles, there are three rather standardized positions all chairs and many decision group members are expected to perform at various times:

Decision group administrator
Meeting head
Official spokesperson and networker for community coalitions (see Exercise 6.2 at the end of this chapter).

Decision Group Administrator. Here, the chair's responsibility is to see that the agenda is out and that the various rules (particularly the rule of halves and the rule of three quarters) are followed. The chair sees that reports are ready and that people with assignments follow them up. This may make the chair into a bit of a nag, but it's necessary.

Frequently, the chair interacts with people outside the meeting to discuss problems they are having, to provide encouragement, even to do a little work here and there. However, although it is helpful for the chair to put his or her shoulder to the wheel, it is harmful in the long run to take over a task. It may be more difficult not to do it all oneself than to perform tasks that members have difficulty with. This requires restraint; it requires toleration of mistakes until people realize that this chair, at least, is serious about assignments once made and that one had better get to them.

As the meeting approaches, it is the chair's responsibility to double-check the meeting room and to double-check all arrangements (or to appoint someone trusted to do so). It's good for chairs to arrive about 15 minutes early at a meeting site to be sure that the door is open. Much time has been lost trying to find janitors to unlock a locked room or trying to find another room because, although the meeting was scheduled for Room 26, someone else has already taken possession of it.

Early arrival also allows the chair to arrange the room properly, to set out refreshments or coffee, or to move furniture if needed. What this communicates to the members, then, is that the chair thinks enough of the membership to take care of details so that serious business can take priority. It encourages members to take matters more seriously when they do not have to spend half their time rearranging furniture or getting coffee.

An oblong seating arrangement with an open center is the optimum arrangement. This highlights the chair at one end and gives everyone a clear view of fellow participants. Of course, other arrangements are possible. A wise idea is to schedule the agenda so there is some time available between the end of your meeting and the next meeting scheduled for that room. This procedure will avoid the confusion of trying to end a meeting while other people are coming in for the next one.

By preparing in advance, the chair can turn his or her attention to greeting people as they come in, chatting, inquiring after this or that, perhaps doing a little work but exchanging pleasantries as well. Frantic beginnings exhaust everyone, even before the meeting has begun.

Rules for a Decision Group Administrator

- Get the agenda out.
- Follow up reports.
- Check on members' assignments.
- Set the stage for the meeting.

Meeting Head. To serve as meeting head—to, in fact, chair—is usually considered the most important of all chair positions. Although running the meeting itself is of crucial importance, of great importance as well is the preparation and position modeling that the chair provides to the decision group.

Principally, running the meeting involves an evenhanded approach, a systematic consideration of the issues before the decision group. This is when items discussed earlier become essential. Agenda integrity and temporal integrity are crucial here. The chair does not participate in the discussion itself but, rather, acts as a discussion facilitator, a clarifier, a mover, and a terminator. Usually, a good way for the chair to focus the discussion is by asking questions such as, "Have we thought of everything on this point?" "Do we want to look into how other agencies accomplish this task?" and so on. (Recall the discussion of decision crystallization in Chapter 5; those ideas apply here as well.)

Rules for a Meeting Head
- Ensure agenda and temporal integrity.
- Facilitate and clarify discussion.
- Move the discussion along.
- Bring the discussion to a close.

Official Spokesperson and Networker for Community Coalitions. Someone has to speak for the decision group. Often, this task falls to the chair. Members expect the chair to pick up this task and represent the decision group fairly. Among other things, this means not using the public media to slant or sway situations. The chair should give some thought to situations in which public statements may be necessary and prepare written versions in advance so that they can be checked with other members.

The chair is the first among equals in the decision group membership but keeps that position only so long as he or she acts consistently with it. If the chair begins to shirk duty, makes too many commitments, does not handle decision group management tasks well, becomes a partisan rather than a statesperson, or is an inadequate spokesperson for the group, the decision group will either find a substitute for the chair or deteriorate.

Similarly, the chair often represents the group in negotiations and networking meetings with other community groups. This function, like the spokesperson's, can be delegated, but the chair needs to retain involvement, because it is through the chair that the official interorganizational work of the group flows.

Rules for an Official Spokesperson and Community Networker
- Voice the decision group's views, not your own.
- Represent the decision group's public image.
- Prepare to meet the media and check your preparations with others.
- Offer to initiate and host community interactions as well as join them.

CONCLUSION

The chair position is one of the key positions in decision groups. Although all does not depend on what the chair does, the skilled executing of this position can make the difference between an excellent group and one that is just passable. Poor performance, on the other hand, can turn any group into a time dump, into which a huge amount of time is poured with no or negative results.

> Marcia thought a lot about the call from Armondo. The first thing she did was to tell him she would need some time to reflect on his offer. That gave her time. "I'm off the hook, not off the cuff," she thought. She spent the next day or so at the library, looking up what various writers had to say about being a chair. She also talked to a couple of women she knew whom she considered to be excellent at their jobs. By the time she finished, she thought she had a good idea of what it took to be a good chair. There were a couple of things she needed to ask Armondo to provide. If she could get the committee's agreement on those, she would accept. She reached for the phone.

EXERCISE 6.1

BEFORE YOU BECOME CHAIR

Consider the following key preacceptance activities:

- The meaning of membership
- The mandate
- Transition to a different position in the group
- Specification of resources
- Specification of staff assistance
- Specification of certain kinds of membership

Have you completed these before you have become chair?

Why or why not?

EXERCISE 6.2

THREE RESPONSIBILITIES OF THE CHAIR

Consider the three main subpositions of the chair:

- Decision group administrator
- Meeting head
- Official spokesperson and networker for community

When you have been chair, have you carried these out well?

Why or why not?

How about a chair you know?

Chapter 7

THE MEMBER

After Armondo finished talking to Marcia, he thought "Boy, I hope she accepts. This job of recruitment is getting me down." In the meantime, across town, the phone was ringing in the home of Sally Smith-Wesson. As she answered, she recognized the voice of Peter Pound, executive of the Community Foundation.

"Sally," Peter said, speaking quickly, "we here at the Community Foundation want you to join our board. There really is not much to it, just a meeting or two a quarter; and the meetings are short! Do say yes!"

Sally had not really had much to do with the Community Foundation. She was worried, though, that Peter's fast-talking, high-pressure tactics would make her uncomfortable. "I will have to get back to you, Peter," she replied. "I am really honored. But I want to think a little about it."

For the member, position acceptance involves an explicit recognition of the tasks that the member hopes and is expected to perform. If, for example, a minority member is expected to represent the minority perspective but that member feels he or she cannot, this issue must be faced before acceptance. Conditions must be assessed at the beginning of candidacy. It is much easier to decline graciously at first than it is to exit later. A little homework done in advance pays great dividends as time moves on.

BECOMING A MEMBER

For the member, conditions of importance can include items such as the following:

Candidate's expected perspective
Demands of time and workload
Dynamics of the decision group

As one becomes a member of a decision group, a number of issues can arise. One issue is to explore what the candidate hopes to accomplish. There should be a sense that the candidate's interests fit with those of the group. Then, too, there needs to be an honest exploration of time and workload. Peter, in the opening scenario, is misrepresenting the demands, a not uncommon recruiting device. But no good is served by lying to potential members about demands of service. Those members will retaliate with nonparticipation and absence.

Finally, there needs to be some discussion of the particular dynamics of the decision group in question. Groups approach things in lots of different ways. Some are more high-powered; some more low-keyed. Some have a diverse membership; some have not yet achieved diversity. These points are important ones to touch on as you consider a membership offer.

MEMBER RESPONSIBILITIES

What does a member do? One person told me that "there is not much to learn about being a member; you show up and doze off. Anyone can do it!" The last chapter considered the chair. But a chair without effective membership is hardly an effective chair. What is expected of the member in all of this? The member's position is complementary to the chair's, just as a musician has a position that complements the conductor's. The member's position involves the following:

Attention to meeting structure
Preparation for meeting content
Service to the decision group outside meeting
Participation in meetings
Respect for decision group purposes

Attention to Structure. It is the member's responsibility as well as the chair's to insist on agenda integrity and temporal integrity. Sometimes, it may be necessary to insist that the agenda be followed, that previously set time lines be kept. In more desperate situations, members may need to ask that an agenda be created and time guidelines established. This is a member's prerogative. It should be unnecessary to add that the member has a responsibility to follow the agenda at the meeting. What is not always known is that members have a responsibility to aid the chair in reaching closure, even to suggest compromises when structural constraints become important.

Preparation for Content. Clearly, the member must pay attention, must read the material and be prepared for participation. Members need to have some information about the material to be discussed and to have time to look over the material and think about it. This opportunity for thought is one of the powerful reasons for the rules of agenda integrity, halves, and three quarters. If the material is not out in time, it is not possible to look it over; and if one cannot look it over, participation is more "shooting from the lip" than anything else. If the material is available, however, as I suggest and hope, then members have an obligation to look over the material and try to have some thoughts about it and reactions to it.

Service Outside the Meeting. The member also has a responsibility to participate outside the decision group in small groups interested in certain subissues. These decisions are then brought to the larger group for final ratification. A member may also act as an intelligence-gathering source, alerting the decision group to trouble spots, matters requiring attention, or areas in which the member has particular expertise.

Participation. Not surprisingly, this is the crucial act on the part of the member, and it is important that the member participate responsibly. Responsible membership means participating fully yet avoiding overparticipation. Either constant intrusion into the conversation or total silence is irresponsible. Members are often unaware that the silent member is seen as the critical member. If you wish to be silent or if you are having an off day, it is extremely useful to simply state, "I'm not going to participate as much today," thereby diffusing a potentially difficult situation. Part of the reason for this is that as time goes on or the silent member becomes more and more dominant through her or his silence. This dominance needs to be tempered.

The member must use some discretion and not create a situation in which there are two functioning chairs; however, participation does include assistance in modifying the positions of other members, in asking for clarification and the opinion of silent members, and engaging in some behavioral shaping of other members who are overparticipating. A member can say something such as, "Steve, I think we've got your point, and I'd like to hear what Harry has to say on this issue. I know that he has some interesting perspectives." If done diplomatically, it will be an effective technique because it permits the chair to support the member rather than to always be the disciplinarian or taskmaster.

Respect for the Decision Group. Finally, a member has the responsibility to be loyal and discreet. This means that confidential decision group business should not be shared with those who are not decision group members, particularly during budget hearings, appropriation hearings, promotion hearings, or any other matters of heightened sensitivity that involve personnel or finance. Members should avoid publicly criticizing the decision group, even though they may privately disagree with it or have advocated a rejected course that the decision group could have used to get out of its current hot spot.

Resist the temptation to say, "Well, I, of course, never wanted to do that. I was always in favor of something different." If a member feels strongly that an alternate direction should be pursued, it is time to resign. And resignation should be offered only in very special circumstances, not, as is too frequently the case, as a tool to secure compliance. I know those who regularly resign, who always get their way because other members fear causing a resignation. If you are a member faced with such a situation, propose that the resignation of that other member be accepted. It is inappropriate to keep offering to resign just for purposes of compliance.

CONCLUSION

Member activities require forethought and planning. One cannot just agree to become a member. There is a need for active engagement. This comes from some exploration during the recruitment phase and a knowledge of what is really expected as you join. These expectations need to be carefully distinguished from what you may be told. Membership, after all, has responsibilities (see Exercises 7.1 and 7.2 at the end of this chapter).

After several calls that Peter did not return, Sally finally got him on the line.

"I have thought about your offer, Peter, and I am flattered. I would like to join you, but I have some questions. I have made a list of them and already faxed them to your office this morning. I'll need to get together with you and Simon (the president of the Community Foundation) to go over them."

"Fine, fine," Peter said, thinking to himself, "She is not going to be as easy to handle as I thought."

EXERCISE 7.1

MEMBER RESPONSIBILITIES

Consider the five main responsibilities of the member.

1. Attention to meeting structure
2. Preparation for meeting content
3. Service to the decision group outside the meeting
4. Participation in meetings
5. Respect for committee purposes

When you have been a member of a decision-making group, have you carried out these responsibilities? Why or why not?

EXERCISE 7.2

RULES FOR MEMBERSHIP

All too often, we do not look into a potential membership or chairship thoroughly enough. Later, we're stuck. If we think about the manifest and latent aspects, we may become more knowledgeable members before we even get on the committee. Think of a recent committee or board you were asked to chair and think of one also that you were asked to join. With these in mind, think about the following rules with the (a) stated, public reasons (manifest ones) in mind, as well as the (b) unstated, private reasons (latent ones).

Some examples of stated public reasons might be these: They needed your skills; they needed your interest; no one else was good; it would take only a little while; and so on. Some examples of unstated private reasons might be these: They needed a woman (minority, person of a certain religious background, whatever); you were the only person who would accept; you are known as a strong (weak) person, and the appointing authority wanted to send a message to some group observing the process.

1. What are the conditions for membership?
   a. Public, stated reasons (and conditions)
   b. Private, unstated reasons (and conditions)
2. What is the group's mandate?
   a. Public, stated mandate
   b. Private, unstated mandate
3. What is the meaning of membership?
   a. Public, stated meaning
   b. Private, unstated meaning
4. What is the meaning of acceptance (to you, to others)?
   a. Public, stated meaning
   b. Private, unstated meaning

Chapter 8

THE STAFFER

Franklin was a little apprehensive about his upcoming meeting with Sol. He was
not sure why, though—just that Sol had seemed upset. Franklin sensed this
when Sol had called to ask him if they could "debrief" the recent allocations
committee meeting that Franklin had staffed. He was new at this staffing stuff,
but it was going great. Why, he had even joined in a vote that resulted in a tie;
now there was another meeting. Franklin wondered if that was what was on
Sol's mind. Perhaps he should have read some of the material that Sol had
given him.

One of the important areas to understand in decision group and board life
is the position of the staff person and the executive person. A staff person
is an individual paid to assist the decision group in carrying out its
functions—not someone on the staff of the agency. It refers to the verb *staff,*
to give staff service to a decision group. Such a person is present at the
meeting and usually has provided a range of services before the meeting
begins. He or she plays a less active position at the meeting itself. This
behavior is in contrast to what the executive usually does (see Chapter 9).

One of the major problems that staffers have—and that decision groups
have with staffers—is that their own views get mixed up with the analyses
they are presenting. This makes it impossible for the decision group to sift
out a set of alternatives not colored by a staffer's often unconscious views.
One suggestion is to make those views conscious by including them in the
options memo. Staffers should practice doing policy options, which I
recommend be three-part memos composed as follows: problem analysis,
presentation of alternative solutions, and staff recommendations.

ROLES AND RESPONSIBILITIES

The staff person is paid to assist the decision group in carrying out its
functions. The staff person *is not a member* of the decision group and does

not have the right to participate as a decision group member. This restricted position is often disliked, particularly by young staffers who feel they have a great deal to contribute and should be heard. I agree that there is a contribution to be made, but I do not agree that the meeting is the place for it.

Their contribution is made by working up documents for decision group consideration rather than by participating in the meeting itself: This would make the line between members and nonmembers very fuzzy indeed. Members resent having a nonmember take sides when that person will not be the one to take responsibility for a favored decision. Staff persons should be unobtrusive at meetings. The staffer makes sure that the mechanics of the meeting have been handled and continue to be handled. This may require taking minutes. Minute taking, in fact, is the chief meeting task that a staff person is expected to perform.

The staffer has other roles and responsibilities. Among the most important are the following:

Resource person
Consultant
Catalyst
Enabler
Strategic and tactical assistant to the chair
Stage manager
Policy loyalist

RESOURCE PERSON, CONSULTANT, CATALYST, AND ENABLER

As a *resource person,* the staffer must be knowledgeable about areas of concern to the decision group. Whether it is a decision group on child welfare or a decision group dealing with employee compensation, the staffer should be knowledgeable about that area.

The decision group should be able to rely on the staff person to update it about the most recent technical and professional thinking in a particular area. In this respect, the staffer is a *consultant* to the decision group, helping the decision group think through alternatives it might wish to adopt. This consultant position, although sometimes expressed in the meeting itself, is not played directly there but, rather, in submeetings or in more individual sessions where the decision group as a whole is not in session.

The staffer can serve as a *catalyst* by providing information and research findings and sometimes through assisting the chair in bringing key individuals together whose joint perspective can open up new routes and approaches for the decision group. Often, the staffer brings information about how other are working on the same problem.

In this respect, the staffer is an *enabler,* doing decision group work that helps that decision group function. The staffer facilitates the group process by undertaking a certain set of tasks so that the group does not have to worry about them rather than stimulating this or that behavior within the group itself. For example, the staffer secures information, gets documents and references for decision group members, takes the directions from the committee (through the chair), and follows up on them. In addition, there is a whole set of housekeeping tasks, such as preparing for the meeting, getting the room ready, and so on.

STRATEGIC AND TACTICAL
ASSISTANT TO THE CHAIR

The effective staffer collaborates with the chair as a strategist and tactician. Because agenda items need to be ordered from easy to difficult to easy, a preliminary ranking must be done by the staffer. The order can then be readjusted or changed by the chair when the two meet. Indeed, it is important that the staffer meet regularly with the chair before meetings, particularly if there are issues pending about which the two might disagree. Such disagreements can be fully and completely discussed in a private meeting, even though they may not be resolved there, but they should not go on in the meeting. It confuses members to be forced to sit through a detailed, in-depth discussion between staff and chair about this or that. Such discussion should occur outside the meeting or in special submeetings.

In working with and assisting the chair, the staff person is responsible for helping to develop meeting tactics. The staffer may

suggest ways to handle items in terms of order and content;
name key interested individuals whose views need to be considered; or
point out opponents, if known, to a particular direction.

These tasks complement the staffer's responsibility to work with the chair on decision group strategy. Together, the staffer and decision group

plan agenda items ahead (for future meetings),
develop a fund of knowledge about items of decision group interest, and
represent news of other decision groups and individuals to the decision group.

Because staffers know a good deal about what is going on in both the community and the agency, they are in a good position to suggest that certain items be hastened or held back. Decisions by this decision group, for example, may be seen as the basis of deliberations coming up in another decision group. It may be more appropriate for Decision Group X (the program decision group) to wait until Decision Group Y (the finance decision group) has acted before it spends a lot of time discussing programs for which there may be no budget. Decision group members and chairs would do well to make effective use of staffers.

STAGE MANAGER

After meeting with the chair, the staff person, at the chair's discretion, is responsible for the details of meeting preparation. Many of these responsibilities would belong to the chair if there were no staff person. Making sure the room is ready, sending announcements out, arranging for parking, and ordering refreshments can be delegated to staffers if they are available. Decision group and board members must be careful not to misuse or abuse staff members whose contributions in other areas may be more important.

Typically, when a staff person is available, it is his or her responsibility to perform many of the stage management aspects of preparation for meetings. But when the meeting itself becomes a reality, the staff person "sits back," playing a subordinate position, taking minutes, and contributing on request. He or she may be more assertive when clarification is needed. If there is a clear point of fact, the staffer must mention it with care. The staffer should heed the spirit of this recommendation, however, rather than its letter. Sometimes staffers can participate more, if the occasion calls for it. If a staffer looks over his or her behavior within a given period and notices a pattern of increased participation, however, it may be time to cut back. The tendency to participate like a full member and even to usurp the position of the chair must be resisted.

POLICY LOYALIST

Like decision group members, the staff person is responsible for policy loyalty. But he or she is also responsible for contributing beyond simple compliance with the goals and missions of the decision group. If the chair does not get that kind of support from a staff person, both chair and staffer may find themselves seeking other assignments. To the chair, a nonsupportive staffer represents a potentially lackluster performance at best and dangerous sabotage at worst. Staff persons are no more comfortable with a nonproductive position. It is difficult to continue to do something that you feel is in contradiction to your own policy orientations. Until this point is reached, however, the staff person should not be critical of the decision group for which he or she works, except in discussions with his or her administrative superior. That is the correct route by which to raise questions about decision group activity. We are frequently asked to carry out missions with which we disagree. If such disagreement is less than fundamental, then a talk with the chair about the ways in which one might carry out the mission in question becomes appropriate.

BOUNDARIES OF SERVICE

The staffer needs to develop a good working relationship with the chair. To this end, an early meeting with the chair, before accepting a staff position, can be very useful. This meeting could be initiated by the chair, but generally the staff person should take the initiative. If it seems that there will be serious strain working with a particular chair, that potential difficulty should be brought to the attention of the appointing authority. Strains are bound to occur from time to time because staffers typically have two bosses. One is the staffer's administrative supervisor, usually the organizational superior and the person who assigns the staffer to the particular decision group. The other is the decision group chair, who usually has authority over the staff person and can direct that person's work and effort for the time the staff has available.

This brings up an important matter. The amount of time available should be decided on as much as possible before staff work begins. Are we talking about 1 day a week, 2 days a week, 3 days a week, full-time, or what, exactly? Decision group work can mushroom: I have been involved in many situations in which staffers have been desperately overburdened but have felt powerless to pull out of the situation, short of quitting and finding another job. The pressures that can lead to resigning usually derive from conflicts concerning how much time is needed versus how much time is available.

When the time needed exceeds the time available, the staff person should have a frank discussion with the chair, indicate what his or her limitations are, and think through with the chair how additional resources might be garnered. If the issues cannot be resolved here, the appointing authority must be consulted. The staff position can demand much time and effort. It is not made any easier by the fact that a staffer may simultaneously hold two or three assignments with two or three decision groups and have two or three chairs to work with, each of whom has a somewhat different style of working. Given such a situation, staffers must keep the work related to each decision group as separate as possible to avoid overlapping.

Rules for Staffers
- Inform and provide consultation.
- Give technical assistance.

- Stimulate decision group activity.
- Promote decision group function.
- Analyze choices.
- Develop strategies.
- Set the meeting stage.
- Serve decision group interests (see Exercise 8.1 at the end of this chapter).

CONCLUSION

The staffer can provide immeasurable aid to a decision group. It is important for the staffer to remember that he or she is a servant of the group, helping it to work well and achieve. Sometimes, staffers forget their position. On the other hand, chairs and members must remember that the staffer is a competent professional who deserves a hearing, who is expected to be knowledgeable and share that knowledge with the group. The staffer is a helper, assisting decision groups in accomplishing their missions, not a "gofer."

As the second meeting with Franklin ended, Sol felt irritated but positive. Franklin was a good kid. Perhaps after today he would really begin to pay attention to the material he had already received. That business about the vote! When Sol heard about that, he about went through the roof. When Franklin had come in for the initial meeting, Sol had quizzed him a bit on the staffer position. Franklin knew less than nothing, if that was possible. Sol sent him away to study and come back. After he had read the material, Franklin saw the problem of voting—and learned some other things as well.

Exercise 8.1

The Staffer Role

Think of a recent meeting where you had someone staff your committee (provide assistance to it). Did that person perform the following tasks?

Role	Performed Yes or No	How Well?
Inform and provide consultation.		
Give technical assistance.		
Stimulate committee activity.		
Promote committee function.		
Analyze choices.		
Develop strategies.		
Set meeting stage.		
Serve committee interests.		

Think of some time when you might have had such a role. Which of these functions did you perform? How well do you think you performed them?

1.

2.

3.

4.

5.

6.

7.

8.

Chapter 9

THE EXECUTIVE

Sally Smith-Wesson and Bea Sharpe were talking about Sally's recent promotion. She had replaced Peter Pound as Executive Director of the Community Foundation. Peter had taken a job at a larger foundation, but there was also talk that he was too directive. Bea had been an executive for many years and was experienced in working with her board and with the staff members of her agency. In addition, Bea had some experience with the Music Therapy Association, as chair. Bea was telling Sally something about the executive position in working with a board.

"What's important," said Bea, "is to change a little bit from when you were a staffer to decision groups. Then, you did research for the group, kept the minutes, and were generally a quiet participant. Now, while you bring proposals to the group, like you did before, you can argue a bit for them."

"I see," said Sally. "But I'm not really a member."

"That is not true," Bea reminded her. "You are an ex officio member. That means you are a member by virtue of your executive position, but you don't have a vote. This is one of the differences between your old position and your new position."

"Well," said Sally, "I hope I do well."

"I'm sure you will," replied Bea. "Keep in mind that you need to work with your board, let them know what is going on, develop a manual or information booklet for their use, and meet regularly with the chair. You'll do fine."

"Thanks," said Sally. "I'm looking forward to it."

In some ways, the executive is a high-level staff person. But even though the executive shares many responsibilities with the staff person, there is a fundamental difference—typically, executives work with boards of directors and staff groups. Their responsibilities are with the central policy-making body of their organizations, whereas staffers may assist a whole range of decision groups, including a board and a variety of subdecision groups. Usually, executives have a central responsibility to "their board." The superintendent of schools plays this position with respect to the board of education. The executive director of a family service agency plays this position with respect to the board of the agency. Someone who is director of a mental health clinic is the "employee" of the board, which hires and fires him. The executive director is an individual who has primary responsibility to a policy-making board rather than to decision groups. Decision groups may recommend policy but may not always have policy-making authority. This makes interaction with boards potentially more serious, and of greater consequence, than is typically the case with decision groups and subdecision groups.

Obviously a discussion of the executive role could take a volume in and of itself. The purpose here will be to deal with the executive's role with one particular, and crucial, decision-making group—the board of directors. Executives can experience many problematic interactions with the board. Some executives think that the board should follow their lead—the "strong-executive model." If the board is weak, as the Community Foundation Board might have been, there is the additional factor of a "weak-board model." Basically, vigorous executives and vigorous boards are a winning combination to handle the pressures that arise in at the agency. If there is not a sharing of mutual strength, the organization may tilt off in one direction or another.

STRUCTURE OF THE EXECUTIVE POSITION

An executive shares responsibility for the mission and position of the agency or organization. Thus he or she is usually a member of the board in an *ex officio* or nonvoting capacity. This pattern of having an executive in a nonvoting capacity is not typical of all sectors. Indeed, one of the powers of the chair came from the fact that the chair was also chief operating officer. This is true, for example, at the University of Michigan, where the president of the university is also the chief operating officer of that university. Large corporations tend to use this pattern as well.

In human services, we are more familiar with the separation of the board and the executive, with the board tending toward volunteer or lay representation of community interests and the executive being the highest-paid professional staff person within the organization (sometimes called the CPO, or chief professional officer). These differences in orientation, background, and overall responsibility can generate conflict. It is part of the executive's responsibility to be aware of these potentials and to work to avoid them.

In recent years, there has been a tendency for executives in the human service sector to adopt the organizational forms of the commercial sector. This approach has meant that the old executive director has become the president. The person who was head of the board of directors, who used to be called the president, has now become chairperson of the board. We are in a time of transition. Some executive directors remain. Some executive directors remain with the same functional responsibilities, but are called president, chief executive officer (CEO), or as I mentioned, CPO. In the United Way movement, there is a lot of variability, but the term *CPO* is frequently used. In some cases, the president is an ex officio member of the board; in some cases, chair of the board. At present (1995), there is no common form. For this reason, I will approach the board-executive relationship from a generic perspective, with the understanding that readers will need to adjust the points, depending on their own particular situation.

POLICY AND ADMINISTRATION

The turmoil in the specific nature of the position of the executive (CEO, CPO, president, executive secretary) is one reason that the old distinction between administration and policy is probably not fully applicable. It suggests that the board makes policy and the executive carries it out. The truth lies more in an amalgam than a distinction. The board together with the executive makes policy and the executive carries it out. The executive also makes policy without the board but within parameters set up by the board. In fact, added to differences in background and responsibility, the fuzziness between policy and administration continually creates difficulties and tensions between board and executive.

It is not possible to clarify these differences completely. In part, that is because there is a "jointness" about the responsibility. The executive, after all, is the one who must carry out the policy decisions. He or she will need the support of the board, and the board will need the support of the person in that slot. As a rule of thumb, items that are of broad scope; that commit substantial agency resources; that involve senior personnel; or that affect the vision, mission, or strategic direction of the organization are policy matters that require clearance with the board.

DUTIES AND EXPECTATIONS OF THE EXECUTIVE

Seven duties seem to be the most important expectations of the executive with respect to the board:

making a professional presentation,
alerting the board to policy issues,
making a case,
working with the board as a partner,
developing and educating the board,
dealing with board sensitivities, and
working with the staff on behalf of the board.

Making a Professional Presentation. This involves the board's expectation that the executive is a knowledgeable, up-to-date professional in his or her chosen field. The executive's duty is broader and more inclusive than the similar responsibility of a staff person. The executive is seen as the professional custodian of the agency and the person who will answer professional questions asked by the board. For this reason, the executive must be alert to professional issues and be ready to educate the board in regard to these as time goes on. Stemming from this professional competence is the second task of alerting the board to policy issues.

Alerting the Board to Policy Issues. Although members of the board and the chair will know of emerging policy issues in the community, the executive is thought to be the key in this function. Like the chair, the executive must develop an intelligence system that brings community issues, staff issues, and issues affecting the agency to his or her attention and then to the board for consideration and action. Similarly, in professional matters, the executive is expected to alert the board to matters of interest developing in the field. New techniques of intervention—for example, new techniques of bookkeeping; new standards; new regulations from federal, state, local, or other sources of review—are part of the kind of information that the executive brings to a human service board.

Making a Case. The executive is entitled to make a case—and is expected to. The authority and expectation stem from the executive's presumed expertise and from the fact that he or she is close to operational concerns.

Working With the Board as a Partner. The executive works with the board in partnership as a colleague who shares with board members in the interests of the organization. This is because the executive and board share "custody" of the organization's mission and role. Although it hires and fires the executive and approves his or her salary, the board hardly regards the executive as just another employee. The board and executive share a tenure that the executive must cultivate. The board sees and must respect that the executive has a longer term, perhaps, than many board members. Thus the executive may have a perspective of history in addition to professional competence. Nevertheless, the executive must accept that the board can go against his or her wishes. Joint responsibility does not mean that things always have to go the executive's way—or the board's way.

Developing and Educating the Board. A special responsibility of the executive is to engage in a process of board development and education. Training as a board activity is discussed in Chapter 11. Here, it is important to stress the job of the executive to teach. Governance is a complex phenomenon, and the executive has wisdom that can be shared, a little at a time, with the board, individually or collectively. On the other hand, all executives should be students, too, and learn from the wisdom of board members.

Dealing With Board Sensitivities. In the human service field, at least, board activities are volunteer contributions. People participate on boards out of a sense of public commitment, public interest, and concern for a particular area, as well as a wish to advance causes in which they feel particularly interested. Executives must recognize that this volunteer aspect requires some attention. Particularly when the executive has had the job for a long period of time, he or she may come to regard the board as an obstacle. This attitude violates the central principle of mission sharing. When either the executive or the board believes that only he or she or only the board has full responsibility, a good working relationship is hampered.

Because we expect that the executive will know more about these matters than does the board, it tends to be the executive's responsibility to be tuned to board sensitivities. For example, executives commonly have stationery designed to feature their names prominently and the board's name in smaller letters, if at all. Lettering should be equal, or out of courtesy, the board's name should be printed in slightly larger type. Trivial as this example is, it represents an attitude or disposition that executives sometimes take toward the board.

Rather than working with the board and educating it, some executives believe the board is to be overcome. To be sure, there are times when such effort is necessary. But too frequently, this perspective is arrived at out of frustration because other kinds of working relationships were never established. When working relationships are well tended and cultivated by the executive, a mutuality and sense of jointness is much more typical.

The executive is also responsible for many of the mechanics of meeting preparation. Often, we find executives grasping for more exalted responsibilities and turning those that appear less elegant over to clumsy and uninterested subordinates. Thus matters of the agenda, the room, the meeting time, and getting packets out may be handled in an unimaginative fashion. Board members may feel slighted or unappreciated. Although they may be silent about their feelings, tensions can be expressed more appropriately in other kinds of board decisions made. Therefore, in any problem between executive and board, I look first at the staffer's part played by the executive to see whether or not it is being handled appropriately (e.g., although an executive does not take minutes, he or she frequently reviews minutes for accuracy and policy appropriateness). Then I move to the larger and more complex duties.

Working With the Staff on Behalf of the Board. The executive is the working liaison between the board and the agency staff. The executive has to interpret board policy to the staff and has to vigorously interpret staff action to the board. This may be a hot spot for the executive, because he or she becomes momentarily disliked by both the staff and the board. That triad, however, needs to be cultivated. One of the best uses of a once-a-year educational or training session is to provide opportunities for interaction between the board and the agency staff. At meetings orchestrated by the executive, the board and the agency staff can be helped to share perspectives and concerns. It is frequently a surprise for each group to hear the concerns of the other group. Boards, for example, often feel that staffers are not committed and are just "out for the buck." Staffers, on the other hand, sometimes feel that boards are removed and remote and don't really care. Many times, these perceptions are wrong on both counts and can damage the development of a relationship of trust.

Rules for the Executive
- Present a professional perspective; offer expertise where needed.
- Keep the board informed of policy issues.
- Work sensitively with the board.
- Offer the board development opportunities.
- Work energetically with the agency staff and link the board to the staff (see Exercise 9.1 at the end of this chapter).

CONCLUSION

Staffer positions and executive positions are difficult and different. The staffer needs to provide a supportive service to the board or decision group, often playing a subdominant role with respect to participation in the meeting, stressing the facets of participation and preparation. Executives, on the other hand, are almost always working with decision-making boards or decision-making groups. This gives their job a somewhat different character, although they do play (with the exception of taking minutes in the meeting itself) the staffer position. There is a jointness to the decision-making functions that occur here, even if the executive does not have a vote. The board has hired that executive to provide professional guidance and perspective. His or her views will be taken into account. When that relationship begins to break down, good decision making becomes very difficult.

As Peter left the meeting of the Community Foundation Board he was stunned. Fired! He never thought it could happen to him. Anger rushed over him, replacing the waves of anxiety he'd been feeling. He could not really think straight. And they had already identified a replacement—Sally Smith-Wesson. He thought about how odd it was that he had just been trying to recruit her to the board; it must have been shortly after that they had talked with her, without saying a word to him! He felt so "ticked." He had wanted her because he felt she would help him get through some of his new ideas, ideas that "OFs" (old farts) on the board were blocking. But he remembered a conversation over lunch a few weeks ago with Dee Flat. She had indicated, informally, that she had heard that some of his board members were displeased with him; they felt he was moving too fast and not bringing them information. Peter recalled replying that boards bored him stiff and indicating that he was the one responsible for moving the agency ahead. Dee had cautioned him that sometimes a good working relationship with a board pays off. He recalled telling her how fired up he was about some new plan. Now he was actually fired. Perhaps he should call her back and see what he should do.

EXERCISE 9.1

The Executive

Think of a time you were on a board. Rate the executive on the job elements discussed in this chapter.

How could he or she have improved? What did he or she do well?
- Making a professional presentation
- Alerting the board to policy issues
- Making a case
- Working with the board as a partner
- Developing and educating the board
- Dealing with board sensitivities
- Working with the staff on behalf of the board

Chapter 10

Roles in Meetings

Jim Zingerman was feeling great as he left the staff meeting. What would they do without him? Once again he had nailed a stupid idea that one of the other staff had brought up. It was a new idea and had not been really thought through. He had pointed out several obvious flaws and said to the group, "Well, as the devil's advocate, it's my job."

Sylvia had been upset, however, and others did not seem that happy either. He was ruminating on these things in the men's room when George walked in.

"Hi!" said Jim, his voice resonating with self-congratulation.

" 'Lo," George replied.

"Something wrong?" Jim asked.

"No," George replied, "except that I am going to have to spend a lot of time with Sylvia to repair the damage you just did. Do you *always* have to play the devil's advocate? Isn't there anything you ever like?"

Jim felt like he had been hit in the face. "Whoa, dude. What do you mean? I did a great service—that plan was full of crap. It had holes in it so big you could drive a truck through them. Listen, wimpface, if it weren't for me, this agency would be full of quarter-baked programs made from half-baked ideas." His reply indicated how upset he was at the challenge—and in the men's room no less.

"Wimpface!" replied George, whose face was not red. "In these meetings you act like Vlad the Impaler. Any idea anyone has you find fault with, and I notice you have none of your own. Oh no, never give anyone the chance to do to you what you do to them. You don't protect the agency from problems, Jim, you destroy new ideas. We are behind the times here, largely because no one wants to face you in the staff meeting, and no one has the guts to tell you that you are an ass. What gives you the right? Who appointed you, to protect us from—whatever."

George stormed out. Jim sat down on the lid of the toilet seat, stunned. Nothing like this had ever happened to him—well, not since his wife left. And come to think of it, it was a sort of similar explosion around some of the same points—her thinking he was so critical, him thinking (and knowing) he was right, that he was just being helpful.

In decision-making groups, we all play roles—whether we think we do or not. A role is a part in the meeting "play." There is the talkative member, the silent member, the devil's advocate, the "nice guy," and so on. Roles are temporary assignments, assignments made by ourselves (we choose the role) or assignments made by others (we are assigned a role—"Will you take the minutes? You do such a good job"). Two points are important. Roles do not need to be permanent. We can change them.

Second, it's good to change them because if we play one role too much, even one that has been assigned, groups apply a kind of discount rate to our performance in them, which, in turn, leads to overemphasis on the role, which, in its turn, leads to further discounting. You can see how this situation could lead to trouble.

KEY ROLES

There are many key roles, but some of the most important are listed here. They tend to come in pairs and, to some extent, balance each other:

Leader/follower
Task role/process role
Devil's advocate/angel's advocate
Interpersonal attender/idea offerer

LEADER/FOLLOWER

The leader sets the tone and direction of the decision group. If someone saunters in late, makes remarks such as, "Well, I don't want to be here any more than you do," engages in numerous side conversations, pokes fun at members, makes subtle racial slurs about other members, and generally presents a behavioral model that is demeaning to the decision group, the decision group could pick this up and act accordingly.

One aspect of leadership is the modeling of behavior. By his or her actions, the chair informs the decision group how he or she wishes it to run and how seriously or lightly he or she considers the group. Actions do, in this case, speak louder than words. Too often, we find that chairs get exactly the decision groups they deserve. In fact, even more to the point, chairs get the decision groups they ask for. Sometimes the language is body language and behavioral language rather than the spoken word. But it is, nonetheless, effective communication.

Leadership also involves political and intellectual synthesis. The chair participates a bit less than do other members because the chair's contribution is more to provide mortar to join different decisional blocks than to provide the blocks themselves. On political grounds, the chair looks for possibilities for bringing about certain types of relationships between members, for suggesting new possibilities of positional compromise, for tempering the behavior of certain members, and for eliciting participation from quieter members to ensure a fair balance of participation.

For this reason, the chair needs to be alert to what is being said, who is saying it, and what the reactions are. This makes it possible to intervene in such a graceful and diplomatic way as to keep the meeting on course. If the chair has a reputation for skill in this area, he or she will be a very much sought after individual. Less stressed, but equally important, is the position of intellectual leadership.

An effective chair hears the ideas that people are communicating—or trying to communicate—and makes an effort to blend the idea of one member with the idea of another member. Here is the place where the chair's contribution may be directly substantive, coming up with a new amalgam that is stronger than any of the original components.

Statesmanship as it applies to leadership is a neutral evenhandedness in which no one individual or group is given preference over another, in which weaker groups are enhanced and stronger groups tempered so that every person and every group has at least an opportunity—although not necessarily an identical opportunity—to present views.

Rules for a Decision Group Leader

- Model decision group behavior.
- Synthesize political and intellectual material.
- Preside in a neutral, statesmanlike fashion (see Exercise 10.1 at the end of this chapter).

The follower provides supportive backup to whoever is leading at the moment. Such backup consists of constructive contributions, in which the ideas of the leader are questioned, tested, and honed. They are also melded with the ideas of others in the group.

TASK ROLE/PROCESS ROLE

A task role is composed of actions in which the player encourages others to think of the specifics of the job to be done, the deadlines to be met, and so on and encourages the group to attend to those items. Sometimes, in playing such roles, individuals move too fast, push the group past and over appropriate steps and processes, and fail to take a broader range of wishes into account. It is a necessary role, but it needs to be mixed with the process role.

A process role looks after the appropriate steps in the process of decision making. Has the proper range of views been considered? Has there been time to think? Has everyone had a chance for input. Approaches such as this are necessary to high-quality group decision making, but they are sometimes viewed as "unnecessary" by the person playing the task role. Of course, both are needed. Balance is the key.

DEVIL'S ADVOCATE/ANGEL'S ADVOCATE

The devil's advocate is a historically recognized role, one that involves the player in asking touchy, difficult, and embarrassing questions, usually tinged with negativism, about ideas on the floor. The devil's advocate is, of course, needed because the enthusiasm of new ideas needs the chilling effect of scrutiny. All too often, however, the devil's advocate applies his or her role to new ideas and leaves accepted ideas without the benefit of this kind of critique.

The role of angel's advocate was introduced in *Entrepreneurial Systems for the 1990s* (Tropman & Morningstar, 1989). The angel's advocate is a role that supports new ideas. It picks up John F. Kennedy's phrase, "Why not?" Obviously, both the devil's advocate and the angel's advocate perform useful functions in the decision group.

INTERPERSONAL ATTENDER/IDEA OFFERER

Groups need someone to perform a role that looks after the feelings of members. This role supports the points of others and sympathizes when difficulties occur. It seeks to protect the weak and keep the strong under control. It rejects those comments that are hurtful and nasty.

As a balance to the interpersonal role, the intellectual role is one interested in ideas more than in people. It seeks to introduce ideas when needed, blends those available with other ideas into yet new ones, supports and questions ideas on the table, and so on. The role has an intellectual focus.

MIXING AND PHASING

Although there are other roles available in decision-making groups, these are among the most important. There are two key points to remember with respect to roles. The first is that, over the course of the group, everyone should play all the roles. No role is reserved for any one person. In this context, it means the necessity of developing a role repertoire and varying the roles throughout the meeting.

How does one know which roles to play? The answer is to offer what is needed. If there is lots of leadership, be a follower. If there is lots of devil's advocacy going on, become an angel's advocate. Seek, in your own role performance, to effect a balance in the decision group. That will help the progress toward high-quality decisions.

CONCLUSION

The playing and the changing of roles throughout the meeting and over several meetings is crucial to the success of the decision group. After all, no one person is the leader, the follower, or whatever. Resist typecasting. Vary your presentation of self so that others do not typecast you and so that you are able to make different kinds of contributions to the group.

For Jim, George's comment had been like an electric shock. Because of his marital situation, he was in counseling, and he raised the issue of George's comment and its meaning with the counselor. But he had already come to the conclusion that he should play different roles in meetings and maybe at home too. Amazingly, the next joint session with his wife went extremely well. As did the one after that. He had changed his behavior. At work, he found a greater sense of acceptance. He apologized to Sylvia and offered to help her work up the idea for another presentation. She and the others could not believe it. There were two good results. One was for him personally. The second was that events in which he was involved—events that had always seemed to be characterized by conflict—began to improve, go better, have better results. "Could it be this simple?" Jim thought. "No way!" he answered himself—but maybe it could be that simple.

EXERCISE 10.1

ROLES IN MEETINGS

Consider the role dichotomies in meetings. Do you play each of these roles within a series of meetings?

- Leader follower
- Task role/process role
- Devil's advocate/angel's advocate
- Interpersonal attender/idea offerer

How can you practice some of the roles that you play only occasionally?

PART III

Different Kinds of Decision Groups

In this last part of the book, the focus moves to different kinds of groups, ones that are typical in the human service arena. Already, some focus on this element has been introduced—the executive position, for example, was discussed mainly with respect to the board.

The most important types of decision groups are

task forces,

the ad hoc and standing decision groups,

commissions,

informal groups,

boards,

advisory groups, and

staff groups.

The first four types of decision groups will be discussed here, and the last three—boards, advisory groups, and staff groups—will be discussed in the Chapters 11, 12, and 13, respectively.

Each of these types of groups performs different functions. Most decision groups are not of a single type. Most are predominantly one type but perform other functions, and when they do, they partake of the characteristics of that type. Decision group functions include the giving of advice, the making of decisions, the gathering of information, and so on.

Task Forces. Unfortunately, most of the groups called "task forces" are really "task farces." A task force should be a group of people with the resources (permission to make decisions, equipment, money, people) needed to carry out some assignment.

A Red Cross Disaster team is a good example. Many task forces are really advisory decision groups.

Ad Hoc and Standing Decision Groups. Ad hoc decision groups should be appointed for a specific mission, with a "sunset provision" that is a given time in which they are expected to go out of existence. Standing decision groups, on the other hand, are ones that have a continual life. Sometimes, assignments (of people or tasks) can be made on a time-lined basis to permanent decision groups. The reason I like ad hoc appointments, even when continuous functions are involved, is that they permit a reassessment of new functions and memberships without giving offense.

Commissions. These groups are usually appointed by some political authority (road commissions, presidential commissions, etc.) to make decisions and, as such, have a political cast to them. Commissions often issue reports and cast their decisions in the form of recommendations or policies that are to be followed up by others.

Informal Groups. What about informal meetings with friends? People tell me, "Your suggestions are fine but surely not for a small church group or for a group of my friends." I could not disagree more. Although it is certainly true that any set of rules needs to be applied with intelligence and discretion, informal groups in which people know each other well are among the most dissatisfying to the members. Precisely because people know each other, they seem to take two, three, or four times as long to accomplish something that strangers could do with dispatch. In part, of course, this lengthened time can be explained by the multiplicity of agendas that always come up when friends get together. My attention, however, has been drawn again and again to the lack of focus, the lack of detailed planning, and the lack of thoughtful preparation that characterizes more intimate decision groups. No physician would avoid giving a proper physical examination to someone just because he or she knew that person as a friend. Similarly, lawyers have a saying that a person who acts as his or her own attorney has a fool for a client. All these speak to the dangers of intimacy and lack of objectivity at crucial moments.

What is suggested here, then, is that one should use many of the procedures for orderly meetings as well as the prethinking and preplanning. A little planning does not hurt; rather, it can help a great deal, particularly in those groups in which planning is thought to be unnecessary and is thus nonexistent.

Chapter 11

THE BOARD

Bill Bland had just gotten a call from the nominating committee of the ABC board. There had been a recent crisis, when he had criticized the current board (and its chair, Frank). He told the board they were all wasting their time if they could not function more efficiently and effectively and serve the community through high quality decisions. Now they had taken his challenge; they had asked him to be the chair!

A board is a legally chartered, legally responsible, decision-making body. Its function is to make decisions. Its procedures, the processes it uses, and the expertise it takes should all be oriented toward that function. Boards should be known for the decisions they make and should be able to make them after appropriate deliberative time. Postmature decisions (taking too long) and premature decisions (deciding too quickly) should be avoided.

MAKING THE RIGHT DECISIONS

As a decision-making group, and one legally and ethically responsible to a range of constituencies for its actions, it is vital that the board spend time on the right topics. This chapter will not present a board guide, because those are readily available (e.g., Carver, 1990; Houle, 1989; Tropman, Johnson, & Tropman, 1992; Zander, 1993). Here, it would be good to emphasize the kinds of decisions the board should carefully attend to. From my perspective, these are

recruitment,
selection and evaluation of the executive,

strategic planning, and
oversight.

RECRUITMENT OF VOLUNTEER MEMBERS

A board of directors is a self-generating body. As such, it has to take great care to recruit appropriately, ensuring that a variety of goals are met and that customers are satisfied. Because of its self-perpetuating nature, there is lots of opportunity for it to "go off the deep end" and engage in a variety of problematic practices, such as self-cloning and keeping people past their term.

Often, the recruitment is relatively thoughtless and accomplished at the last minute. There is a better way to recruit board members and a better way for recruits to consider whether or not to accept the invitation. There are also more effective ways of orienting and training recruits. All three areas are important. Together, they can contribute to more effective decision group participation and management. I will suggest a number of rules for how those positions should be performed.

Recruitment is a process, not a moment. I recommend what I call *phased* rather than the typical *episodic* recruitment. In phased recruitment, new members are appointed or elected to decision group or board membership only after some prior experience with the organization. This experience may be as a volunteer, a participant in a subdecision group, someone involved in a fund-raising effort, and so on. Some boards have many decision groups on which new prospects can "test their mettle," a bit like players in the bush leagues. Some make it to the majors; some do not. But those who do are ready to play. Some organizations establish groups such as the Friends of the XYZ Agency. Such a group may meet infrequently, perhaps annually, but it is briefed on a regular basis about the activities of the organization.

Their members are asked periodically to do special tasks for the board: investigating this or that, representing the board at some special function, and so on. In this way, mutual exploration helps the potential board member weigh the activities of the organization in more detail without having to make a 3- or 5-year commitment to board membership. Individuals in this "friends' group" may even be invited to join the board in some self-training activities, if that is seen as appropriate by the board. The board can also see whether this or that individual's interests and competencies represent the orientation desired by the board. After a suitable period, perhaps a year, the candidate can be invited to membership.

Recruitment to the board comes from an outer circle of participation that surrounds the board, not strangers who are brought into the "inner sanctum" but people from this in-between or way-station group. One is recruited to the bush league group rather than the board.

Rules for Phased Recruitment
- Identify potential candidates.
- Involve candidates around their interests or on special tasks.
- Recruit candidates for full membership.

The same procedures used in phased recruitment to a board or committee can be used in "internal recruitment," where officers are selected and elevated on a phased-in or graduated basis. Membership on the board is the preliminary stage, followed by a succession of posts of increasing responsibility leading to a presidency or vice presidency. There is a great deal to be said for such conventional procedures as setting up a line of succession in which the vice chair or chair-elect assumes the chair the following year. This assures that knowledgeable individuals are moved into key leadership roles.

SELECTION AND EVALUATION OF THE EXECUTIVE

There are several problems with the search and evaluation process when selecting an executive. The whole process of search and review can be made easier if a few matters are attended to first. Among the more important of these is setting up a contractual period for the hiring of the executive. Often, 3 to 5 or 6 years is a good contractual period. If it tilts toward the longer time period, then a specific major evaluation should be done midway, and this requirement also should be written into the contract. Yearly evaluations should be done, and some procedures for them should be specified. It is important to be this specific because it's always easier to set up procedures for positions when there is no person in the position. This set of requirements can then be an integral part of the considerations used by the candidate. All too often, executives stay because no one knows how to get rid of them. It should be added here that executive turnover is not always due, or even often due, to incompetence or bad performance. It is more frequently due to changes in the goal structure and direction of the organization or changes in the desires on the part of the specific executive for a larger or smaller or different role for himself or herself. We all recognize that people have different skills, and frequently, the skills of a particular executive meet organizational needs at a specific point in time but don't meet them at some later point in time. There ought to be a way to assist that executive to move to a job in which his or her skills are more appropriate and to secure someone who has the skills for the present phase of the agency's development and activity.

Part of the way this goal is accomplished is to link the term of the executive with the major policy review and refurbishment schedule. It's been suggested that every 7 years a major assessment of the organization should occur. This could be a period when goals might be readjusted. If the contract of the executive is tied in with that schedule, then it becomes possible to make an adjustment in the position of executive director at the same time and consistent with an adjustment in goals. Often, if the former is not done, the latter will not occur even though formal change in mission and role has been approved by the board.

It is also necessary to be aware of any legal requirements that the organization must follow in thinking about a new executive. Some of these are specified in the bylaws and outline specific procedures that must be followed to make the search and selection process legal and legitimate. The organization must also be sensitive to any public laws (local, state, federal) that govern the search process.

Often, it is possible to secure help with both search and assessment from national agencies or special firms. For example, United Way of America and the United Way of Canada both provide assistance to local United Ways in the search process, and it would be useful for local United Ways to confer with representatives from those central organizations before directors set about the job of selecting a new executive.

The search process can lead into and set the stage for the process of evaluation. It has already been suggested that there should be an evaluation policy in place that specifies a contract period and requires regular evaluations. It is most useful to have such evaluations yearly, although other time periods can be used if they seem appropriate to the agency or organization in question. The important point is to sit down and talk through accomplishments and failures during the year. This process is made easier, however, if there are two periods rather than one.

A system that often works well begins the evaluation process with a discussion of the goals that the executive in the organization seeks to achieve during the year. These will be operationalized versions of the larger mission and role statement of the organization (and the annualized goals) and represent agreed-on trajectories of activity for the organization and the executive. Often, it is useful for the president to ask the executive to set down a list of achievements that he or she hopes for during the coming year and their links to organizational problems and strengths. The board or the executive committee may then look at this memorandum, accept it, make revisions in it, and, usually, talk with the executive about it. Through that talking process, a mutually agreed-on set of activities for the year develops.

This becomes important because the executive's accomplishment depends, to a large part, on the activities of others, not excluding the board itself. Hence board members need to be aware that insisting on some objectives for an executive might require their involvement in a variety of ways, and they have to be prepared to commit those resources. In any event, a document is agreed on, and that document provides the basis for assessment at year's end. Often, the president will sit down with the executive and go over the list of goals in an effort to cover the successes and the problems. Prior to the evaluation meeting, a self-assessment from the executive may be requested and the president and the board may prepare, using the same chart sheet, their own assessment. These two assessments can then be compared, with commonalties and differences noted and discussed.

There are, of course, other ways to approach evaluation, but this two-step process, which involves setting up a set of targets and then measuring the progress toward those targets, is among the better ones that boards can use. In part, it is the two-step aspect that adds strength, because all too often executives do not know that the board wants them to accomplish something other than what they are aiming toward. This results in premature termination. But any system can be used. The point is to have a system and to use it annually.

Regular reviews of the executive mean that such goals and objectives can be specified. Then one can talk with the executive about whether they have been met or not (see Exercise 11.1 at the end of this chapter).

STRATEGIC PLANNING

An overall assessment process and strategic initiative allow a more global, in-depth picture to emerge of the kinds of activities the organization is undertaking, along with the costs and benefits of these activities. SWOT analyses are relatively common in the strategic-planning field and, in any event, are likely to be used by consultants.

A SWOT analysis is really not very complicated. It involves analyzing the agency from four differential perspectives: Strengths, Weaknesses, Opportunities, and Threats. Teams of directors and staff, and other volunteers who might be interested, are assigned to review the agency's position vis-à-vis these four variables. One team reviews the organization's strengths. What are its strong points? What is it known for, today and in the past? How might these strengths be capitalized, extended, or converted to new purposes? These and other questions are asked of the strength assessment group.

A weakness team is assigned to think about the problems that the organization is facing. What are the points of difficulty, the areas of low quality, the areas of trouble? Particular care must be taken here to be honest, open, and direct. Every organization, like every person, has strengths and weaknesses. Organizations, like people, tend to overstate their strengths and minimize their weaknesses. Indeed, to listen to many individuals in organizations describe themselves, one would think that the weaknesses were either infinitesimal or nonexistent. Clearly, personal and organizational defense mechanisms are at work here—and powerfully so. These need to be set aside for SWOT analysis; otherwise, at a report conference, the individuals receiving the weakness team report will not have a fair and honest idea of what is really troubling the organization.

A third team looks at opportunities in the environment. What opportunities might be available for this particular organization? Are they being exploited now, or could they be exploited in the future? Is the environment changing in a way to make new opportunities likely? For example, in the college and university area, it is well-known that following a baby boom comes a "baby bust" with fewer students in the college-age bracket. Naturally, colleges and universities will seek to expand the fraction of those individuals of college age who come to university or college. It is also possible, however, and indeed desirable, to redefine what "college age" means, anyway. Many universities aggressively seek the older student, the student in his or her 30s, 40s, 50s, or 60s who has a yearning for an education that was not completed at an earlier age or who simply seeks to expand the knowledge base that he or she has at that particular moment in time. It is an exciting adventure. But one needs to see the opportunity in the older student before one can pursue it.

Finally, organizational threats are assessed by a fourth team. What is it in the environment that looks like it might harm the organization? Have government allocations become increasingly uncertain? Has a particular residential treatment center, run by an agency, had a string of troubles and difficulties that have caused the attention of accrediting groups to swing in the agency's direction? Is there an ominous decline in individuals interested in working for the agency at the wage rates currently available? These and other questions represent an analysis of the threats facing the agency. They naturally link up with weaknesses, and if there is an unfortunate confluence of threats and weaknesses—that is, if the threats to the agency seem to come in its area of weakness—then the agency is in a perilous state.

There is no special formula for carrying out these analyses, although the large number of materials available on strategic planning suggest a variety of ways to approach it. The main point is to do it. After the analysis has been completed, agency members come together, often in a retreat format, to discuss the findings and to plot new directions. Presumably, new directions arise out of a consideration of strengths and opportunities on the positive side and from a scrutiny of threats and weaknesses on the negative side. One seeks to neutralize threats and reduce the effect of weaknesses while augmenting strengths and seizing opportunities. This small exercise can really help an organization to avoid trouble and difficulty in the process of self-renewal.

It is very difficult, however, to undergo strategic planning every year. The process becomes tiresome and unproductive. Therefore, the organization should try to establish, on an annual basis, a strategic review. As boards enter the strategic planning process, it is imperative that they think through the requisites of such a process. The first step is to review the strategic blending of perspectives and requisites so that there is a common understanding of the kinds of energies that will be required and a common agreement to set aside presuppositions, predefinitions, and simple solutions and adopt a readiness to explore new opportunities, with this review as a beginning point. Although many tools are available to assist in strategic planning, the first step is to develop a basic readiness. Without that original readiness, it is not going to make much difference what techniques you use; progress will not occur.

OVERSIGHT

Part of what a board needs to do is a regular review of ongoing programs. This oversight is essential, but boards need to remember that it is not appropriate to "micromanage" the programs. Reports should be avoided and the board should look at questions and issues with respect to programs.

BOARD DECISION GROUP FUNCTIONING

Let us now step back for a moment and recall some reasons why decision groups are portrayed in such a bad light. Why do they seem to have such difficulty accomplishing their purposes while, at the same time, they are of such importance to modern society? What problems must the decision group cope with as it goes about its business?

Typically, decision groups are burdened with two levels of mission. Their immediate mission is to make a set of decisions around some specific topic. But decision groups serve society and their varied organizations in a much broader way. An understanding, then, of their functions is essential for a proper perspective of the modern-day board.

Rules for Board Decision Group Functioning
- Equalize participation.
- Demonstrate preference.

- Represent social diversity.
- Express diverse opinions.
- Balance conflicting values and perspectives.
- Influence others (see Exercise 11.2 at the end of this chapter).

Equalize Participation. Boards function to enhance quality in American life. They represent one of the subsystems of our large society in which different types of people can come together; particularly, they provide an opportunity for those who might have not enjoyed the full fruits of society to enter into the decision-making processes that affect them. Perhaps nowhere is this clearer than in the attempt within Johnson-era poverty programs to insist on "maximum feasible participation of the poor." It was recognized quite broadly that those who were disenfranchised in one sector of the society were also disenfranchised from the decision group and the boardroom.

Because much of significance went on in those rooms, the planners felt that the poor and the disadvantaged should have their say. Very little, of course, was done to prepare them for these positions—new, for many. Nonetheless, the intent was to use the decision group process to enhance one of the values that we cherish. This function is an important one for boards, but it adds difficulty to their tasks.

Demonstrate Preference. Effective boards serve as vehicles through which the intensity of preference can be expressed. The typical way in which democracies make decisions is to vote. Even in grade school, when the teacher wants to know how many want to stay inside for recess, the students raise their hands. The majority rules. This is well accepted. Yet the problem it presents is of a very practical nature: People are differentially affected by these decisions, and we have no good way of expressing that preference. Some people feel very strongly about a small range of issues and care very little about most of the other issues.

Yet we all get to vote on all of the issues set before us in the polity. This is perhaps the reason our society has developed the decision group: as a mechanism by which a person's intensity of preference can be expressed. If you are particularly interested in some area and get to work on boards that work in that area, you will have, by informal agreement, greater say in what goes on. Decision groups, then, perform a very important function for the decision-making structure of the society, much as the outrigger on a large canoe balances the canoe. This function, too, complicates decision group activity.

Represent Social Diversity. Apart from equalizing participation and demonstrating preference, boards are also expected to promote pluralism.

We all like to think that boards represent the full range of interests, so frequently we will try to get a man, a woman, a black, a white, a Protestant, a Catholic, a Jewish person, a businessperson, a labor leader, somebody from uptown, somebody from downtown, somebody from the east side, or somebody from the west side to be sure that all of the different components of the decisional framework are represented. That boards are expected to have a diverse membership makes the job of decision processing more interesting but more difficult. Decisions made by boards are sometimes faulted because the diversity of the decision group is deemed insufficient. Thus a third function links to a fourth—the expressing of diverse opinions.

Express Diverse Opinions. Boards are frequently seen as "mini" legislatures with "official" representation from the black community, women's groups, the Jewish community, and so on. This, too, can be problematic because the individual selected informally for one of these positions may not want to be the representative of a particular group. It may be that the minister or monseigneur or rabbi does not want to or cannot speak for the Protestant community, the Catholic community, or the Jewish community but would just like to be regarded as a person with interests and a contribution to make. This tension between representation on the one hand and representativeness on the other becomes one of the enduring tensions of the decision group.

We always seek people who can play a dual role—to speak for themselves and for their community. Sometimes this works; often, it does not. The problem is compounded when we have knowledge that the individual definitely does not speak for the community, but the individual insists that he or she does. At that point, a series of complex decision group maneuvers is often undertaken to supplement the view of the nonrepresentative individual so that the full range of his or her community's perspectives can be laid before the decision group.

Balance Conflicting Values and Perspectives. The more complex the society, the more we expect boards to serve as vehicles for balancing conflicting values, both within ourselves and within society. The day of the single, heroic, unconflicted organizational decision maker is probably past. Doubtless, there are companies and communities where a single unconflicted purpose still dominates. But in the main, problems are too complex, too multifaceted for this to be true. A particular decision involves too many considerations for one individual or one view to completely dominate. How much can one person know and retain? How many implications can be processed by a single individual? How free is that individual from fatal bias? Frequently, these questions are all answered in the negative. It is just not possible for an individual to be knowledgeable or, for that matter, sufficiently powerful to make all necessary decisions. Thus boards come into play. Boards are designed to enable a range of knowledge or expertise to be brought to bear on a problem. Sitting around the table, one can have people from finance, law, the executive suite, the secretarial cadre, and so on, each of whom may have a particularly crucial piece of information about a particular aspect of the decision. Singly, theirs are partial contributions; jointly, they represent the sum total of components needed not only to make a decision but to make a good decision. Complex society is decision group society whether we like it or not. But the need to have information and to have the appropriate range of information represents one of the difficulties with which boards must continually deal.

Influence Others. Finally, boards represent, despite all of their bad press, the locus of power. Boards in communities and organizations represent the place where the formal power structure and the informal power structure get together. If one wants to find out who is running an organization, few studies would be more productive than a study of its decision group structure. Positional power individuals, who hold informal positions, use a perspective developed by C. Wright Mills (1956) that can be supplemented by Hunter's (1953, 1980) reputational authority (i.e., seen by others as powerful) to provide a list of formal and informal leaders.

TRAINING

The common task of both members and the chair is to be sensitive to what is actually happening in the decision group meeting itself and in the decision group process outside the meeting. Indeed, none of these suggestions is overly striking when taken one by one, but each, if ignored, represents a major archetype of decision group difficulty: the overparticipator, the underparticipator, the person who is never prepared, the person who arrives late, the person who threatens to resign, and so on. Unfortunately, each of these difficulties is all too frequently perceived as a pathological manifestation of the offending member's personality.

Too rarely do we look at the operation of the decision group itself and ask whether, for example, there are supports for enhancing the participation of the silent member or if other members seek to temper the overparticipator. Generally speaking, attention to structure and to preparation for both the members and the chair pay handsomely in terms of more interesting, more fruitful meetings, meetings in which tasks are accomplished and the integrity of the individuals is retained. It is toward this goal that the chair and members should work.

Most people, however, do not have the background and education in group decision-making procedures because our society has not really emphasized that setting as an important one. Japanese society, as a contrary example, has paid more attention to this need. Reischauer (1978) comments, "If the Japanese have a special decision-making process, it is the system of careful and extensive consultations before a decision is arrived at by general consensus." In contrast with Westerners, he notes that "the cooperative nature of the Japanese decision-making process makes it difficult for Japanese companies to utilize foreign executives" (p. 188).

American society, then, tends to ignore preparation for the variety of positions within the group decision-making process. Decision group activity operates on a catch-as-catch-can basis. I recommend something different, a more regularized and rationalized approach to membership in decision-making groups. Typically, such activity is called "training," although the phrase "education and training" would be more appropriate, because it includes broader aspects or perspectives.

Let us talk about training, first noting that what follows applies to boards specifically and decision groups generally. Boards simply tend to be more permanent and ongoing.

For boards, there should be a minimum of a training session once a year, what some organizations call an "educational day" for board members. This can help boards and executives (and fellow board members) get to know each other better. Here, new materials about the mission and role of the agency can be shared. A set of such materials could be discussed. Think of how little opportunity there is for board members, as opposed to staff, to meet to discuss their developmental needs. Boards should take the initiative, if their executives do not, to advocate some small portion of their resources to a board development fund. Confer with the executive on how this fund might be generated or allocated. Also, consider special sessions for new members in which they are oriented to board member responsibilities. Three principles deserve emphasis.

Rules for Training

- Legitimacy: Training is a legitimate board (group) enterprise.
- Right to training: Each member is entitled to support for self-development as a decision group member.
- A board or decision group manual is a crucial training tool (see Exercise 11.3 at the end of this chapter).

Legitimacy. Most boards approve in their budgets an item for membership development. They expect the executive and the staff of the agency to take advantage of this to conduct professional meetings, to deliver reports about the agency's programs, and so on. It is very rare, however, that the board makes any provision for such development for itself. This is because it may not conceive of itself as needing development. I believe nothing could be farther from the truth.

Both for individual members and for a decision-making group, growth is always possible and desirable. Boards can start out with a yearly group activity that involves development and a yearly individual activity. The whole matter of board recruitment, in fact, begins with a package of activities involving board training that supports (a) the concept that boards, too, can grow and develop and (b) the conviction that their members have a right to—and an obligation to participate in—this kind of benefit.

The Right to Training and Development. Each member would be entitled to apply to the agency for support for some type of activity generally related to his or her development as a board member. This is the least we can do for the voluntary service provided by many of the board members. A possibility might be meeting around a particular topic. It might be a subscription to some kind of magazine or other periodical. It may be anything, as long as an appropriate, designated official approves it and there has been a preliminary OK for money in the budget for such matters.

The Board Manual. Any board also needs to give thought to the more explicit training of board or decision group members. An individual who is the recruitment chair or nominating decision group chair should have among his or her responsibilities the designing of a board manual laying out all bylaws, practices, habits, and conventions that are followed. This can be made available to new members. Such a manual can be regularly updated. It should represent more than just the bylaws and a few past minutes. Rather, it should include a codification of the way that particular organization, at the board level, does things.

Most organizations have something equivalent to a standard practice guide, a set of rules and procedures, a codification of policies that is available through the executive director. Such a handbook or pamphlet usually details the various policies, practices, and procedures that have been approved and are current in the agency. It is also available to the staff so that both the staff and the executives can have some sense of what to expect and what rules to enforce. Typically, the board does not have such a pamphlet or handbook available for itself, suggesting our ambivalence toward boards. At one of the crucial levels of the particular organization, the very decision-making level itself, people are too often left to drift this way and that, without any particular guidance.

The creation of such a manual should not become a straitjacket inhibiting the "free spirit" of board members. In my observation, much of this so-called free spirit is a substitute for not knowing what to do. Guidelines more often free us from ignorance than impede us. Some kind of board manual should be available for every board, and it represents an important and legitimate tool for orienting new and prospective members as well as for educating existing ones. It is the type of document that one can present to someone interested in a particular board and that can convey to that individual a sense of what the board is about.

> Bill sat back and thought about his recent term as chair of the ABC Board. His criticisms had, in the previous year, brought him to the chairship. Frank, the friend who had so inaccurately recruited him to the board in the first place, had been very angry at him for his criticism. But Frank had just left, having come over especially to congratulate him on a wonderful year as chair and to talk about Frank's chairship of the board manual subdecision group. Meetings had gone well; decisions had been made promptly and had held up in ensuing months; a process of recruitment had been begun, with visitors coming to the board to get some sense of what was happening. They had even had a retreat during which they talked about goals for the future. Frank had said, "Bill, your chairship has really been an eye-opener to me. I had no idea that meetings could be any different from what I knew. That book *Ineffective Meetings* was very helpful. I have started to use some of that stuff at work, and it is really helping!" Bill felt good.

CONCLUSION

Boards have a range of responsibilities and challenges. Many have viewed board membership as a token activity, of which little was expected and little was given. But in the 1990s boards became more active, taking a vigorous strategic interest in the direction of agencies. This greater activity has led to enhanced interest in the functions and roles of boards, their responsibilities, an understanding of the difficulties they face, and ways that their operations could be improved.

EXERCISE 11.1

BOARD FUNCTIONS

Consider the four functions of boards. How well does a board you are on perform them?

- Recruitment
- Selection and evaluation of the executive
- Strategic planning
- Oversight

Review the evaluation system used for the executive director.

- Is there one in place?
- Is it satisfactory?
- Does it conform to the ideas suggested here?
- How could it be improved?

EXERCISE 11.2

RULES FOR BOARD DECISION GROUP FUNCTIONING

Consider the rules for board decision making.

- Equalize participation.
- Demonstrate preference.
- Represent social diversity.
- Express diverse opinions.
- Balance conflicting values and perspectives.
- Influence others.

How well does your board meet these goals? Why or why not? How could weaker areas be strengthened?

EXERCISE 11.3

RULES FOR TRAINING

Consider the rules for training boards.

- Training is a legitimate board (group) enterprise.
- Each member is entitled to support for self-development as a decision group member.
- A board or decision group manual is a crucial training tool.

Does your board make provision for each of these? Why or why not? How can the situation be improved?

Chapter 12

THE ADVISORY GROUP

Sam and Ed walked out of the Mental Health Advisory Decision Group meeting in Capitol City.

"Good Lord," said Ed. "To think we came all the way from University City for this!"

"I know," said Sam. "I still can't believe it."

What Sam and Ed were talking about related to the processes of the most recent meeting. Their group was to advise the new director of occupational health on a fresh, new state health plan. When they arrived, they saw secretaries wheeling typing chairs loaded with paper into the meeting room. There were three to each chair, one pushing and two holding, because the stacks of paper were high. The director apologized, but said she could not get the report run off in time. The secretaries passed out page after page of a 100-page report, and the decision group members collated it. While that went on, a number of members were trying to do some private business involving funding with the director, each warily eyeing the others.

Finally, the stuff was passed out, and the director said, "Well, why don't you take a few minutes to look this through, and then you can give me your reactions and advice."

Sam had then indicated that it was impossible to do that because they could not read a document of that complexity in a few minutes. The director said that she needed reaction right away because she was seeing the governor later in the day.

One very important kind of group that is very characteristic of the human service community is the "advisory group." But it is frequently misunderstood and misused. On the surface, its functions seem clear enough: The advisory decision group's function is to give advice. But problems arise so frequently with this group that special attention is appropriate.

ADVISORY GROUP CONSIDERATIONS

The advisory group is constructed to provide *advice* to an *advisee*. The two main problems surrounding the advisory group center on these two elements. There is often a question of what advice really is.

The first thing to keep in mind is that the advisory decision group should produce a coherent and intelligent piece of advice, carefully considered and acted on by the decision group as a whole. Although ad hoc discussions on one or another issue can certainly be useful, informal discussions should in no way be thought of as substituting for a coherent advice package.

A second kind of problem deals with the issue of the advisee. Often, the advisee unintentionally presents problems for the group. If he or she is a high-status, high-profile person, it becomes an issue of how to manage such a person. If the person is not actually there, one might wonder how to give advice to an absent advisee.

The advisory decision group often includes a fairly high-status "advice seeker." This person, an executive of an agency, perhaps, is frequently the chair of the decision group providing advice. The chair-advisee may bring along assistants, secretaries, and so on. This immediately creates a situation in which the decision group is overwhelmed by numbers and influence. It is very difficult, for example, for a member of an advisory decision group to say something critical to a prominent advisee. It is even more difficult when that advisee is flanked by assistants, associates, and others in, perhaps, even larger numbers than the advisory decision group membership itself. This is especially so when the advisee tosses out some fast-breaking, late-developing items for the decision group to consider. Different members will comment now on this aspect, now on that. The advisee may conclude by saying, "Thank you very much. This has been most useful and most helpful."

This brief scenario illustrates a key problem that can happen at an advisory decision group meeting. Let's formulate some rules with which we can manage advisory decision group functions more adequately.

MISSION AND ROLE

The first rule for an advisory decision group is to clarify its own functions. These tend to include one or more of the following:

advice,
review, or
approval,

Some advisory groups can give advice only to a designated advisee. Other advisory boards have some additional power because they must review certain materials—although not approve them—before action can be taken. For example, a state agency might be required by law to establish an advisory decision group to review a development plan and comment on it before it can go forward. Seeing and commenting on the development plan does not mean that the advisory decision group must approve it. They do, however, have power to refuse to see a particular plan, and in that way they can effectively block action.

Some advisory boards play an advise-and-consent role in which their approval is necessary. This ratification function gives the decision group considerably more authority.

What differentiates advisory groups from, say, boards is that they do not make the decision. Their function is to comment intelligently on the decision made or to be made by others. The advisory decision group is evaluated on the basis of its advice, not on whether its advice is taken. Many advisory decision groups spend long hours lamenting that they have no "power," and seek to seduce, induce, or otherwise influence the advisee to do what the committee wants.

WRITTEN ADVICE

After the decision group determines exactly what it can do and what it must do, it should require, as an operating norm, that all its advice be given in writing. That means that the advisory decision group will review a concern, formulate news, and crystallize those views into majority or minority views. If appropriate, it will vote and communicate its advice in writing to the advisee. This advice must be the decision group's collective judgment, not a series of independent, individual judgments. Each piece of advice conveyed to an advisee should have been voted on by the decision group. The advisee may be informed whether the vote was unanimous or whether there were substantially different points of view. Where significant differences exist, a minority report is quite legitimate. A majority report accompanied by some minority emendations, however, is quite different from a hodgepodge of individual views. Following the rule of coherence is crucial.

Rules for Getting It in Writing
- Review
- Formulate
- Crystallize

- Vote
- Communicate

AN EX OFFICIO ADVISEE

Regardless of the traditions in a given community, it is better if the advisee is not chair of his or her own advisory group. It is virtually impossible to exercise the position of chair appropriately when the group's advice is going to you. The advisee should always be an ex officio member, one who sometimes sits in to share information or provide explanation, and, of course, because advice will be put in writing, the advisee need not always be present to receive advice. Because advisees are usually relatively high-status types, it is almost impossible to avoid contamination of the decision group deliberations. Objective advice is best given when discussion can occur without the advisee's presence. Conclusions can be drawn and communicated thoughtfully in writing to the advisee for his or her own review and consideration.

WRITTEN RESPONSE

The advisory decision group should always request its advisee to respond in writing. In this way, the advisory decision group can know specifically what it was that the advisee did or did not like about the advice, what he or she found helpful or impossible to accept. Advisees, of course, will not be totally candid in all instances with their written responses. Some may not wish to provide them at all. Nonetheless, it is extremely helpful if this practice can be established because it structures the interaction between the decision group and the advisee in a particularly useful way. It answers the complaint, "We never know why the advisee did (or did not) follow your advice." It also induces the advisee to be open and honest with the decision group, clearly laying out the reasons for action.

ASSESSING ADVICE

Because many advisory groups are rarely expected to do much more than participate in "bull sessions," no group consensus is ever arrived at. The quality of the advice given is hard to assess. The advisory decision group may not even know what advice it gave the advisee. If one presses the point and asks, "Look, you're an advisory decision group to Mr. *X,* and I'm one of the constituent members of your group. I'd like to know what kinds of advice you're getting together to give Mr. *X*," the weaknesses of the bull session style of advisory decision group activity become apparent. One never really knows what advice was given because there really was no advice.

On the other hand, if the written model is followed, the answer to that question is fairly straightforward. "Well, we have had a number of discussions, and they have crystallized into several pieces of advice. I would be happy to provide you with copies of our report if you would like to see it." The written advice and the response to that advice are essential to the decision group's ability to evaluate itself. At the end of the year, several members of the decision group should get together to review all their pieces of advice together with the responses to that advice. This will permit decision groups to look seriously at what they did, consider in depth the response they received, and compare the two.

The bull session is nevertheless useful when the decision group is asked to share preliminary ideas that the advisee would like to try out. In effect, the advisory decision group might have a dual focus: a long-range focus that weighs activities of a more thoughtful nature and a practical focus commenting on day-to-day ideas brought by its advisee. Some of these day-to-day issues will emerge as topics for a longer study. The real problem is how to keep these two very different types of agendas from interfering with each other. I recommend the split-agenda technique.

THE SPLIT AGENDA

The split agenda suggests dividing the decision group meeting into two parts. The first part of the meeting considers the range of items and formulates written advice. During this period, the advisee need not always attend. By prescheduling, the advisee can be invited to attend approximately halfway through the meeting.

This does not violate the nature of the agenda structure discussed earlier. The agenda structure can be used for the first half of the meeting. After the break, a "for discussion only" format in which the advisee is present provides opportunity for informal explanation and advice giving.

It is possible, and often desirable, to invite the advisee to comment on various kinds of ongoing matters as well. This can take place in two ways: through the oral meeting process that I just described or by inviting the advisee to respond to a preliminary draft of the written piece of advice. In this way, one can get a feel for the advisee's position without becoming overinvolved.

General Rules for an Advisory Decision Group

- Give thoughtful collective advice.
- Put the advice in writing.
- Request a written response.
- Meet independently for many of the deliberations.
- Review work regularly.
- Meet with and without the advice.
- Check carefully for minority views.

CONCLUSION

Review the general rules just listed. These overall guidelines will immensely improve the work of the advisory decision group. People will feel better about the decision group; they will have a sense of achievement. They will be able to see the effects of the advice that they have given because it is written and because there will be, at least in some instances, written responses to it.

Sinclair Westfield had also been at the meeting of the Mental Health Advisory Decision Group. As he drove home, he thought about how things could be made better. As a prominent physician, interested in the well-being of people in the state, he was troubled that the advisory decision group never seemed to get anything done. Although today was worse than usual, the meetings were usually less than useful. He made a note to call Sam Cohen and Ed O'Brien that evening to see if they couldn't get together and come up with some ideas for improvement.

EXERCISE 12.1

THE ADVISORY GROUP

Advisory committees are responsible for the following activities. Think of an advisory committee you have been on and assess whether or not it has met these requirements. How could it improve?

- Give thoughtful collective advice.
- Put the advice in writing.
- Request a written response.
- Meet independently for many of the deliberations.
- Review work regularly.
- Meet with and without the advisee.
- Check carefully for minority views.

Chapter 13

THE STAFF GROUP

Sheila and Brenda walked out of the family agency staff meeting in a downcast mood.

"I don't know why we have to spend this time every week," said Sheila.

"I don't either," said Brenda. "Nothing ever seems to happen. We complain, we bitch, we moan, the executive gets mad, and we never seem to accomplish anything."

"Didn't Bill actually suggest that we meet every other week at the very least?"

"Yes, that's true," replied Brenda, "but then others said that it was 'good to get together.' "

"I don't think it's 'good to get together,' " Sheila said. "I think it's just a terrible waste of time. If you add up the cost of everybody sitting around there—thirteen of us at $25 an hour—that's a lot of money, week after week after week. Isn't there anything we can do?"

"I don't really know," replied Brenda. "I don't really know."

One of the most common yet troubling regular meetings held by human service organizations (and many other organizations, for that matter) is the staff meeting. When asked about the staff meeting, many executives say, "We have it every week. We always have." But the question really is, "Why do we have it every week?" The answer is probably best expressed in one of the opening lines from *Fiddler on the Roof.* In his song about traditions, Tevye sings of the importance of tradition but admits that he doesn't know *why* his people have their traditions. That's certainly true for most of the staff meetings. They're driven by habit and routine, and people really do not have a good sense of why they're at the meeting.

Based on the material developed in this book, the staff meeting should, in most cases, be canceled. It doesn't serve the purposes of deciding or discussing important organizational matters. Rather, as my opening vignette suggests, it becomes simply a time for people to ventilate, to "schmooze," to have coffee, and in many ways, it becomes a sort of social or quasi-social affair. The problem with the situation is that every so often serious stuff is brought up, perhaps by the executive, perhaps by a staff member. There's then a subtle change in the nature and character of the group, but because no one acknowledges that the group in fact has several different functions, these important items are then not attended to, not followed through on, not dealt with.

A better solution than canceling the staff meeting might be to turn it into an actual decision group.

THE STAFF MEETING AS A DECISION GROUP

The first step in turning the staff meeting into a decision group is to identify the issues around which the staff is being gathered. Most staff meetings are personnel driven—that is, people feel that it's "good to get together." Thus the meeting is scheduled around the people present rather than being driven by the issues that the organization needs to address. The antidote to this situation is to prepare a charter. The charter outlines the mission and role of the staff group. It clarifies the ranges and kinds of issues that should come before it, and it specifies the kinds of results that are expected. This charter preparation will force both the executive director and staff members to honestly confront their expectations.

On the one hand, executives often approach the staff meeting as a ritual. They do want to get staff input, but they're not sure how to get it or whether the staff meeting is the best place to get it, and they generally treat the staff group as an advisory committee, except in those instances where they ask the staff to take a more active role. These expectations, however, are almost never communicated to the staff.

On the staff side, many of the staff people feel that, somehow, they should be deciding issues. But there is also a deep feeling in many staff groups that the executive director has already decided issues and is simply using the staff group as a rubber stamp.

These conflicting perspectives are confounded by the trapped feeling that both executives and staff members have that the meeting series should continue and their common ignorance about what is expected with respect to the issues at hand.

If the executive reorganizes the staff group from the points of view suggested here, he or she will prepare a charter. The first step in charter preparation is to invite staff members to share with the executive the kinds of things they think would be helpful to discuss at such a meeting series.

The invitation asks for categories of items—various kinds of policies and procedures, innovations, and treatment concerns. These are then organized into categories so that when the rule of halves is applied (readers will recall that the rule of halves is that practice whereby individuals are asked to submit items to an agenda in advance) staff members will have some sense of the kinds of issues that ought to be submitted. That will clarify one problem: What comes up at these meetings?

A second problem is what happens to those things that do come up? It is very helpful if the executive director can clarify for the staff different categories of issues from the executive's point of view. This categorization relates to the role that the executive sees the staff group as having with respect to a particular issue. Let me give some examples. Level 1 is an issue about which the executive says, "I have already decided this. I am announcing it here for your information; I will be happy to engage in exchange about it; but I would like the exchange to be within the context that decision X is made." If an executive lays out the issue in this way, there's no confusion, the staff understands that a decision is made—they may not be totally happy about it, but at least there's no pretense that the decision is still open when it is not.

An executive may, however, say something else, such as the following: "With respect to issue Y, I would like to announce that I am going to make the decision, but I would very much like your input on the alternatives that I am considering. I won't promise to follow any of those, in particular, because I have my own thoughts, some of which I'll share here, but I do want your thoughts." In this second, Level 2 approach, the executive is reserving to himself or herself the right to make the decision on the one hand but on the other hand is making it clear that input is wanted and expected, and it is appropriately contextualized so that there is no misunderstanding about how the input is to be used.

A Level 3 request might be something like this: "I am about to make a decision on P. I would very much like your reactions to the different alternatives, and I will be guided by your views as I make my own decision." This approach is distinguished from Level 2 in that the executive indicates to the staff group that he or she will do more than simply listen to the views of the staff but, rather, will take them into explicit (as opposed to implicit) consideration when the time comes for decision making.

There's also a Level 4. An executive may say to a staff group, "An issue is before us that I would like you, the staff group, sitting here, to decide. But I would like to give some parameters from my point of view. The decision needs to fall within these kinds of constraints of time and money. Within that, you can proceed as your judgment dictates." In this approach, the executive director is clarifying for staff members that (a) they can make the decision and (b) the decision needs to be within the parameters just outlined. This is also very helpful to the staff.

Finally, in a Level 5 request, the executive may say to the staff, "An issue has come before us. I would like you, the staff group, to make the decision. It's within your area of expertise, and please let me know what you do." Here, the executive director is allowing the staff to proceed.

Basically, the staff meeting is a unique meeting, because of the interplay of power between the executive director on the one hand and the staff on the other. It is not so much the issue of differential power that is problematic; rather, it is the lack of clarity, issue by issue, about how the executive feels with respect to his or her disposition on that issue. Thus a simple clarification, as just outlined, will go a long way, when combined with a charter to make the staff meetings productive, interesting, and useful to the agency.

Rules for Staff Meetings

- Have a charter.
- The executive should clarify how he or she feels an issue is to be approached (see Exercise 13.1 at the end of this chapter).

INITIATING ADVICE FOR THE EXECUTIVE

The discussion so far has been centered around charter development, a mutual activity between staff members and the executive, and executive clarification. A third important element, however, is staff initiation of points of view. The nature of power relationships in many agencies gives the executive director a lot of ability to control the agenda, even with a charter, and there may be issues that the staff would like to call to the executive's attention that the executive does not initiate. The rule of halves allows everyone access to the agenda, and staff members can raise issues, particularly in the discussion section of the agenda (Item 6 in the agenda bell) and at least inform the executive about the staff's concerns and views. In this respect, the staff meeting is like an advisory group. It is important to emphasize that staff members ought to be able to initiate advice, perspectives, and points of view and have these be part of the agenda. There is, however, one important caveat—staff views do not mean the view of one staff person. If an individual staff member has a perspective that is not shared widely by other staff members, that person can, and perhaps should, communicate that perspective directly and privately to the executive. That is not a meeting item; staff members should not use the meeting as a place where personal views are cloaked in collective legitimation. Thus the staff—and each staff member—needs to be sensitive about the extent to which particularistic views take on universalistic meaning within the staff group itself.

CONCLUSION

The staff meeting can be a useful and powerful tool for organizational development, for the sharing of views, and for a variety of kinds of decision making within the agency shop. Three problems tend to bedevil the staff meeting: (a) lack of charter, (b) lack of clarity on the part of the executive about what he or she really wants from a particular item and his or her disposition with respect to particular items, and (c) uncertainty on the part of staff members about whether they can initiate points view. The solutions here are to prepare a charter, to clarify executive dispositions with respect to each item, and to legitimate and, indeed, encourage staff initiation of points of view. Following these three (relatively) simple approaches will go a long way toward improving staff meetings in social agencies.

At coffee in the workers' lounge, Barbara and Sheila were talking.

"You know," Barb said, "I can't believe how much better our staff meetings have become since we began that new system. Where did that come from?"

"I don't know," her friend replied. "I think one of the other staff members picked it up at a workshop. But our executive bought it, and she seems much happier, too."

"Well, I guess it's a good principle of helping, that when everybody's clear about what's supposed to go on, it makes a big and positive difference."

"Well, it certainly did here."

EXERCISE 13.1

THE STAFF GROUP

Staff groups are supposed to (a) have a charter and (b) work with their bosses to clarify their expectations around issue formation at staff meetings. Is this the case in your staff meetings?

How could they be improved? (Don't forget to think about the rules for meeting performance in Chapter 5 too!)

PART IV

Special Topics

The whole field of effective decision making is changing rapidly. One of the most important areas for all groups to consider, regardless of the kind of group, is evaluation. That material is discussed in Chapter 14.

In addition, some thoughts on developing a perspective are shared in Chapter 15. I stress that the importance of group decision making will only increase and that everything we can do to prepare for it will be to the good.

Chapter 14

EVALUATION AND ACCOUNTABILITY

This book has focused on making decisions and improving decision-making systems. But the question remains, If the process is improved, is the output any good? In other words, are the decisions high-quality decisions?

PROCESS ASSESSMENT

There are many ways to assess whether people are satisfied with the meetings they attend. Many of them are quite complex, but in the main, the focus should be on the process of the meeting itself. That is important. For purposes here, I would like to offer a simple, and effective meeting assessment tool—KSS. It stands for "keep, stop, start." That means that participants are invited, at the end of a meeting, to suggest what the meeting should *keep on doing,* what the meeting should *stop doing,* and what the meeting should *start doing.* It is not complex, it is easy to do, and it tends to focus on actions rather than blame. It is a great way to evaluate meetings, and if you do it every meeting, any initial "sting" will quickly pass.

DECISION ASSESSMENT

The assessment of how people feel about the meetings, however, leaves another element to be considered: What about the decisions themselves? How is the decision group to know whether or not its decisions were good? You can't answer that question without proper records, because no one, yourself included, can remember what you have done. Foremost among them are crisp, clean minutes. Relevant documents should be attached to them. Appropriate revisions should be noted in those minutes. The findings of subdecision groups should be communicated in writing. Together, these records provide the basis for the evaluation of explicitly recorded decisions.

When we evaluate a decision group's functioning, we will not evaluate whether the coffee came on time or whether the meeting room was well ventilated. Certainly, these are crucial. They are necessary but not sufficient conditions, or preconditions, for good decision making. Rather, it is the decision itself that is to be evaluated. My suggestion is that the minutes be culled toward the end of the year for a list of decisions that can be put into an annual or summary report.

It has been my experience that these decisions will fall into several areas of concern, that there seem to be some unifying themes. Decisions, then, can be organized by "theme," listed, and rated. I suggest a scheme for rating that uses standard academic marks, or grades A, B, C, D, and F.

An A decision is one that seemed to improve the situation for all concerned, although not necessarily equally. A B decision is one that resulted in overall improvement, but there were some important winners and losers. A C decision is one that resulted in some lost ground, but there continue to be some winners and some losers. The C decision is the typically partisan decision in which one says, "I'm going to get mine regardless of what it costs you or others." A D decision is one that resulted in everyone's being worse off than before the decision was made. An F decision is a D decision with the result that the decision group ends up being fired.

Decision groups can develop other rating schemes. The only advantage in this one is that it takes a system we are used to using, puts it on one side of the paper, lists all the decisions on the other, and asks for an intelligent grading of the decisions that have been made. This scheme represents two improvements over anything else available. One is that it requires decision groups to do what they often do not do—list decisions. The process itself leads to evaluation. Second, it suggests that thoughtful judgment be applied, in retrospect, with the new information now available.

The annual review of decision group activity is an essential part of planning for the next year. Frequently, one can get out a statement of operational goals framed in the first or second meeting, put that against the overall mission statement, and then look at the set of decisions taken and ask the question, Overall, has any progress been made toward our goals, or has it not? That kind of question is an essential one for the next round of decision group activity. If it is asked, that next round will be even better than the previous one.

Rules on How to Assess
- Use KSS for each meeting.
- Use decision assessment mechanisms for longer time periods.
- Gather minutes and other documents.
- Summarize and review.
- Grade the decisions that have been made.

The accountability aspect of decision group and board life is hard, of course, to enforce. All too often, people are rewarded for bad performance with more decision group assignments! This is best avoided, in my view, through the evaluation and grading procedure. Any procedure will be fine, as long as it involves

systematic recording of decisions (which means making them in the first place!);

a systematic assessment, after time has passed, of those decisions; and

a modification of decision group procedure and of member and chair practice based on that assessment.

Improvement, not punishment, is the goal to seek.

CONCLUSION

Evaluation of both the meeting and the results of the meeting are important elements in creating high-quality decisions. Almost nothing improves by itself.

On the meeting side, the KSS framework—keep, stop, start—is a very useful end-of-meeting tool. It is simply a sheet that asks the members what was good and should be retained, what was less good and should be phased out, and what was not done that should be initiated. The use of this system will keep improvements ongoing and thus reduce the need for major overhauls in meeting structure.

Evaluation of the meeting itself, however, tends toward process thinking rather than results thinking. Use of the decision audit and autopsy is therefore helpful. This approach focuses on decisions and actions as the "product" of the meeting and on stakeholders as the relevant "customers" to be considered. Attention there will pay great dividends.

Chapter 15

DEVELOPING A PERSPECTIVE

This conclusion will seek to pull together some of the perspectives offered in this volume and suggest some overall considerations for those interested in the decision group process, recalling some of the material from the beginning of the book in a way that will suggest a perspective for the future on group decision making and help you frame your own ideas and outlook.

BETTER QUALITY
DECISIONS ARE THE GOAL

First, I would like to emphasize that the goal of this book is to make people more aware of the group decision-making process and their positions in it. Use it to develop your own perspective. In turn, this awareness, it is hoped, will lead to better quality decisions. Decision quality is too rarely considered in thinking about the decision group and board process. Yet that is what it is all about, really. We get together to make decisions. Naturally, if the process is as chaotic as it often seems (and is!), then those decisions will be good due only to chance. I believe that this process can be improved. Through preparation, forethought, and the application of selected techniques, the decision-making group can begin to make decisions from the start. This right action in decision group and board will, I am sure, amaze some and surprise others. Once decisions begin to be made, then the task of improving them can begin.

PERSONALITY OF THE PARTICIPANTS
IS NOT THE MAIN CAUSE OF TROUBLE

Much of the time, we focus on the personalities of members as one of the main causes of problems in decision groups. This diagnosis places blame squarely in the hands of an Arthur Angry or a Tommy Talkalot. There is also a happy consistency with the American ethic of individualism. Surely, personality contributes something here. But as I have emphasized in this volume, the decision group process and the board process are group efforts. Blaming one person is like blaming one worker on an assembly line for a car that does not run right. We need to look at the structure of the positions, the extent to which people know their positions, the extent to which they have position flexibility and can switch from one position to another, and so on. Once these elements are taken into account and we are satisfied that they have been improved, then work on one or two troublesome members can begin.

THE MEETING IS THE END,
NOT THE BEGINNING, OF THE PROCESS

All too often, people who think about ways to improve meetings begin their work at the meeting. That's like trying to prevent conception by talking with the unwanted child after he is born. Much work, as I suggest, needs to be done before the meeting begins. The decision group and board process is like an iceberg, with the meeting as its tip. The direction that tip travels is dictated by the massive understructure of the iceberg; the way the meeting goes is similarly dictated by what has, or has not, gone on before. The meeting is the public performance of the decision group, and one can look at what has been done before to see why that performance is a success or a bomb.

PLANNING AND PREPARATION ARE PART
OF A PROCESS THAT FREES, NOT CONSTRAINS

American society is not planning oriented. As many observers have pointed out, we tend to play the "sleeping giant" role, waiting until some crisis or other develops before moving massively to do something about it. Whether it's family planning, social planning, urban planning, or board planning, we seem to find planning difficult. Somehow, planning gets identified with a restriction of opportunities. "Let's play it by ear" is a frequent phrase. "Conflict never hurt anyone; it clears the air" is another that comes up again and again. There *are* times when one wants to work with a minimum of structure or permit some conflict to clear the air. As a general rule, however, my experience suggests that conflict is often the result of confusion and lack of information and that playing it by ear is not a sensible way for the decision group/board orchestra to operate. One gets cacophony, not a concert.

Planning and preparation so that people know what to expect and can prepare themselves for it decreases the likelihood of poor decisions. Items in the agenda, such as "for discussion only" items, permit a time when discussion can be free-flowing but around preidentified topics. Reports are structures designed to highlight the matters to be decided and to suggest options. Decision-making groups work best when they can build a decision structure from among a series of decision suggestions or decision elements based on work done outside of the meeting. They are not good when they are required to operate in ways that do not give them the information required. Planning and preparation identifies these elements, develops alternatives, and provides, thereby, grist for the decision group mill.

Conflict, is useful to a degree. But conflict and tension need to be managed effectively to keep them from becoming the primary elements within the group situation so that the making of decisions does not become secondary. The agenda structure itself, through the scheduling of items in a bell-shaped curve, provides a way for managing conflict. Indeed, it recognizes conflict and suggests that for conflict to be effective, it must be handled at a period in the meeting when there is the physical energy, the psychological energy, and the attendance to process it.

THE IMPORTANCE OF GROUP
DECISION MAKING WILL ONLY INCREASE

Because demands for goods are increasing and resources are diminishing, the need for group decision making can only increase in the years to come. In addition, as problems become more complex and technical, as many different types of knowledge are required to solve them, then group decision making will increase. Finally, because products are the result of many hands rather than a single pair of hands, the owners of those hands need to get together to talk about how the final product can be improved. It seems to me that a program of improving group decision-making structure and skill can only be helpful. Rather than looking at one more decision group as an additional burden to take one away from "work" (which is always done alone), we should try a perspective in which such situations are seen as opportunities for improvement and try, through these techniques and others, to maximize their utility, to make that next meeting worthwhile not only to you but to others as well.

REFERENCES

Carver, J. (1990). *Boards that make a difference.* San Francisco: Jossey-Bass.

Cohen, M., & March, J. G. (1974). *Leadership and ambiguity.* New York: McGraw-Hill.

Cohen, M., March, J. G., & Olsen, J. (1972). A garbage can model of organizational choice. *Administrative Science Quarterly, 17*(1), 1-25.

Goffman, E. (1959). *The presentation of self in everyday life.* New York: Doubleday.

Goodman, P. S., & Associates. (1986). *Designing effective work groups.* San Francisco: Jossey-Bass.

Hackman, J. R. (Ed.). (1990). *Groups that work (and those that don't).* San Francisco: Jossey-Bass.

Harvey, J. B. (1974, Summer). The Abilene paradox. *Organizational Dynamics,* pp. 63-80.

Houle, C. O. (1989). *Governing boards.* San Francisco: Jossey-Bass.

Hunter, F. (1953). *Community power structure.* Chapel Hill: University of North Carolina Press.

Hunter, F. (1980). *Community power succession.* Chapel Hill: University of North Carolina Press.

Janis, I. (1983). *Groupthink: Psychological studies of policy decisions and fiascoes.* Boston: Houghton Mifflin.

Ketchum, L., & Trist, E. (1992). *All teams are not created equal.* Newbury Park, CA: Sage.

Mills, C. W. (1956). *The power elite.* New York: Oxford University Press.

Reischauer, E. (1978). *The Japanese.* Cambridge, MA: Harvard University Press.

Schwartzman, H. (1989). *The meeting.* New York: Plenum.

Tichy, N., & Devanna, M. A. (1986). *The transformational leader.* New York: John Wiley.

Toffler, A. (1980). *The third wave.* New York: Bantam.

Toffler, A. (1990). *Powershift.* New York: Bantam.

Tropman, E. J., & Tropman, J. E. (1987). Voluntary agencies. In A. Minahan (Ed.), *Encyclopedia of social work* (pp. 825-842). Silver Spring, MD: National Association of Social Workers.

Tropman, J., Johnson, H., & Tropman, E. (1979). *The essentials of committee management.* Chicago: Nelson-Hall.

Tropman, J., Johnson, H., & Tropman, E. (1992). *Committee management in the human services.* Chicago: Nelson-Hall.

Tropman, J. E., & Morningstar, G. (1989). *Entrepreneurial systems for the 1990s.* Westport, CT: Quorum.

Vail, P. (1989). *Managing as a performing art.* San Francisco: Jossey-Bass.

Wetlaufer, S. (1994, November/December). The team that wasn't. *Harvard Business Review,* pp. 22-26.

Zander, A. (1993). *Making boards effective.* San Francisco: Jossey-Bass.

SUGGESTED READINGS

Benedict, R. (1946). *The chrysanthemum and the sword.* Boston: Houghton Mifflin.

Braybrook, D., & Linbloom, C. E. (1963). *A strategy of decision.* Glencoe, IL: Free Press.

Daft, R. (1992). *Organization theory and design* (4th ed.). St. Paul, MN: West.

Janis, I. (1989). *Crucial decisions.* Glencoe, IL: Free Press.

Janis, I., & Mann, L. (1977). *Decision making: A psychological analysis of conflict, choice, and commitment.* Glencoe, IL: Free Press.

Jay, A. (1976, March/April). How to run a meeting. *Harvard Business Review,* pp. 43-57.

Johansen, R. (1988). *Groupware: Computer support for business teams.* Glencoe, IL: Free Press.

Kahneman, D., Slovic, P., & Tversky, A. (1982). *Judgement under uncertainty: Heuristics and biases.* New York: Cambridge University Press.

Kleindorfer, P. R., Kunreuther, H., & Schoemaker, P. J. (1983). *Decision sciences: An integrated perspective.* New York: Cambridge University Press.

March, J., & Simon, H. (1958). *Organizations.* New York: John Wiley.

Marschak, J. (1964). Decision making: Economic aspects. In D. Sills (Ed.), *The international encyclopedia of the social sciences* (Vol. 4, pp. 42-55). Glencoe, IL: Free Press.

McCaskey, M. (1982). *The executive challenge: Managing change and ambiguity.* Marshfield, MA: Pitman.

Morita, A. (1986). *Made in Japan.* New York: Dutton.

Plous, S. (1993). *The psychology of judgment and decision making.* Philadelphia: Temple University Press.

Quinn, R., Rohrbaugh, J., & McGrath, M. R. (1985, November). Automated decision conferencing. *Personnel,* pp. 49-58.

Sayles, L., & Chandler, M. (1971). *Managing large systems.* New York: Harper & Row.

Simon, H. (1960). *Administrative behavior* (2nd ed.). New York: Macmillan.

Sims, R. (1992). Linking groupthink to unethical behavior in organizations. *Journal of Business Ethics, 11,* 651-652.

Thurow, L. (1986). *The management challenge.* Cambridge: MIT.

Tropman, J. E., Erlich, J., & Rothman, J. (Eds.). (1995). *Tactics and techniques of community intervention* (3rd ed.). Itasca, IL: F. E. Peacock.

Tuchman, B. (1984). *The march of folly: From Troy to Vietnam.* New York: Knopf.

Weick, K., & Roberts, K. (1993). Collective mind in organizations: Heedful interrelating on flight decks. *Administrative Science Quarterly, 38,* 357-381.

ABOUT THE AUTHOR

John E. Tropman received a BA in sociology from Oberlin College, an MA in social work from the University of Chicago, and a PhD in sociology and social work from the University of Michigan. Currently, he is a Professor of Nonprofit Administration in the School of Social Work and an Adjunct Professor in the Organizational Behavior and Human Resources Development Program in the School of Business at the University of Michigan. He also teaches in the Executive Education Program at the University of Michigan Business School and in the Executive Education Program at Carnegie Mellon University. He is President of High Quality Decisions of Ann Arbor, Michigan, which specializes in assisting nonprofit executives, their boards, and their staffs improve the delivery of their services and operate effectively and efficiently.

He is an author and editor of many books and articles, including *Strategies of Community Organization* (now in its fifth edition), *Tactics of Community Organization* (now in its third edition), *Public Policy Opinion and the Elderly, American Values and Social Welfare,* and *Entrepreneurial Systems for the 1990s.* With his father, Elmer J. Tropman, he wrote *Committee Management in the Human Services* (now in its second edition).

He presents and consults widely on issues of effective group decision making, transformational leadership, and organizational governance. He also works to help organizations think through strategic planning and total quality approaches, identify their own cultures and organizational styles, and achieve fit between program design, organizational design, and strategy.

He and his wife, Penny, a social worker in clinical practice, have three children—Sarah, Jessica, and Matt.